Train
Your Mind
for Peak
Performance

Train Your Mind for Peak Performance

A Science-Based Approach for Achieving Your Goals

Lyle E. Bourne Jr., PhD,
and Alice F. Healy, PhD

American Psychological Association • Washington, DC

Published by
APA Life Tools
750 First Street, NE
Washington, DC 20002
www.apa.org

To order
APA Order Department
P.O. Box 92984
Washington, DC 20090-2984
Tel: (800) 374-2721;
Direct: (202) 336-5510
Fax: (202) 336-5502;
TDD/TTY: (202) 336-6123
Online: www.apa.org/pubs/books
E-mail: order@apa.org

In the U.K., Europe, Africa, and the Middle East, copies may be ordered from
American Psychological Association
3 Henrietta Street
Covent Garden, London
WC2E 8LU England

Typeset in Sabon by Circle Graphics, Inc., Columbia, MD

Printer: Edwards Brothers, Inc., Lillington, NC
Cover Designer: Naylor Design, Washington, DC

The opinions and statements published are the responsibility of the authors, and such opinions and statements do not necessarily represent the policies of the American Psychological Association.

Library of Congress Cataloging-in-Publication Data
Bourne, Lyle Eugene, 1932-
    Train your mind for peak performance : a science-based approach for achieving your goals / Lyle E. Bourne, Jr., PhD and Alice F. Healy, PhD. — First edition.
        pages cm
    Includes bibliographical references and index.
    ISBN 978-1-4338-1617-8 — ISBN 1-4338-1617-2 1. Mental efficiency.
2. Cognition. 3. Learning, Psychology of. I. Healy, Alice F. II. Title.
    BF431.B63165 2014
    153.1'5—dc23

2013023268

British Library Cataloguing-in-Publication Data
A CIP record is available from the British Library.

Printed in the United States of America
First Edition

http://dx.doi.org/10.1037/14319-000

To our families, in appreciation for their
unconditional love and support:
the Bourne family, Rita (Yaroush),
Barbara (Anderson), Elizabeth, and Andrew
and
the Healy family, Bruce and Charlotte

CONTENTS

PREFACE

There are a lot of books out there on training the body to enhance performance. Fitness training, bodily exercise, good nutrition, and the importance of staying physically active are prominently written about in the media today. However, there is relatively little information on mental training, which is just as important for health and well-being as physical training. Furthermore, mental training can enhance your performance and help you learn a variety of skills. What is the best way to train your mind? In this book, we provide practical tips to help you train your mind and enhance performance on particular kinds of activities or tasks.

The tips we provide are scientifically proven. Indeed, we have researched this topic for about 30 years in the scientific discipline known as *cognitive psychology*. Cognitive psychology is the study of mental processes related to perceiving, attending, thinking, language, and memory. Specifically, we have researched how the activities people carry out in their head can affect their behavior. Through years of experiments, we have learned a lot about how the mind works and what conditions lead to the most effective mental training. This book translates the scientific findings into easy-to-understand tips that anyone should be able to follow. In addition, it provides several miniexperiments that permit readers to test the training tips firsthand and verify that they work. Our hope is that this book will help you improve your mental performance to achieve whatever goals you have set for yourself—whether the goal is learning a new skill, becoming an expert at an existing skill, or maintaining your current level of performance.

There is one caveat to bear in mind. After decades of research, we and others have found that mental training is pretty specific to the task you train on. Training on one mental task probably won't make you an expert at another task. Thus, this book is unlikely to raise your IQ or make you an all-around mental genius—sorry about that! However, it will help you to improve your performance on the task you choose—in sports, in music, in art, or in your job. By following the tips in this book, you will maximize your training and learn how best to acquire and retain knowledge and skills and transfer them to new situations.

ACKNOWLEDGMENTS

Since the mid-1980s, we have been engaged in a cognitive psychological study of training in a variety of domains, ranging from second-language learning through the preparation of first responders in emergency situations to military personnel engaged in the modern networked battlefield. We have had the good fortune to be supported in this work by a variety of funding agencies, including the Army Research Institute, the National Science Foundation, and the National Aeronautics and Space Administration. Most of this research was planned and conducted by us, with the able assistance of many research assistants and associates at the Center for Research on Training at the University of Colorado. We recently concluded work on a 5-year grant from the Army Research Office that allowed us to form a consortium of coinvestigators, similarly interested in training cognition but working in other laboratory settings at Carnegie Mellon University, Purdue University, and Colorado State University. These coinvestigators broadened our effort, bringing expertise in aspects of the training enterprise such as computational modeling, molecular components of skill, automation, and individual differences, which heretofore had been lacking. The accomplishments of this research team have appeared in over

Acknowledgments

100 publications in professional journals, but perhaps most important, in a research monograph titled *Training Cognition: Efficiency, Durability, and Generalizability.*

We thank James Kole for composing most of the illustrations in this volume. We also thank Maureen Adams and Beth Hatch of the American Psychological Association Books Department, who gave us extensive and extremely useful feedback about what to include in the volume and how to structure it; Tim Curran for composing the figure on event-related potentials; and David Strayer for providing the distracted driving photograph. We are also deeply indebted to our many students and collaborators at the University of Colorado and elsewhere who helped to shape the ideas expressed here but are too numerous to list by name. We also profited from the thoughtful and insightful comments and suggestions of the anonymous reviewers whose help was enlisted by the publisher. A lot of the examples cited and exercises described in the text came from studies included in the bibliography.

xii

Train
Your Mind
for Peak
Performance

CHAPTER I

WHAT'S THIS BOOK ALL ABOUT?

Training is everything

—Mark Twain, *Pudd'nhead Wilson*

Let's be clear from the outset. This book is about training the mind. It's about achieving better—possibly expert—mental performance in some activity of everyday life. For example, you might be interested in learning to play a musical instrument, or you might want to learn a new foreign language for an upcoming trip. You'll improve your chances of succeeding in these endeavors if you train your mind properly.

Training the mind is more than just keeping the mind active, important though that is. It's also more than just doing puzzles periodically. As a matter of fact, the effects of puzzle practice are quite limited. Doing a lot of crossword puzzles might improve your ability to do crossword puzzles in the future, but it's unlikely to have any large or general benefit for mental activity. So what *does* training the mind involve, and why should you do it? Basically, training the mind involves practicing a skill under certain conditions so that you learn it well. The goal is to optimize your performance of that activity.

Does training the mind mean that the body is irrelevant? Of course not. When it comes to performance, the body is necessarily involved in expressing the contents of the mind. For example, in expressing your musical knowledge and skills through playing an instrument, performance will always entail bodily action. However, the mind will direct your body, and by that pathway, mental training will enhance your performance. The idea of training is to become the best you can be at your chosen task.

What exactly do you learn when you train your mind? Well, among other things, you learn facts and skills. A *fact* is a piece of information about the world, and a *skill* is the ability to do something with that information. Facts make up your knowledge of the world, and skills enable you to use your worldly knowledge. So, one goal of training is to add to your fact and skill repertoire. The more you know and can do, the better you perform.

Facts and skills are learned in different ways. You can learn a fact by having a single experience. You see (or hear, or feel) something, somebody tells you something, you read something, and then you know it. Thus, facts can be learned rapidly. But facts can be forgotten (or become inaccessible) just as rapidly. So knowledge of facts is an all-or-none thing; either you know the fact or you don't. There are certain things you can do during training to reduce the likelihood of forgetting an important fact, and we discuss some of those techniques in this book. These techniques derive from principles of good effective training.

Skills, in contrast, come with practice, repetition, and drill. Rarely can a skill be acquired in a single practice attempt. Exercising the skill over and over again is the key to skill acquisition. As you practice, execution of the skill will become easier. You'll do it more smoothly, more rapidly, and with fewer errors. You will find that paying attention to what you're doing is very important when you first start out. But with more and more trials of practice, your attention can drift away to other things without jeopardizing your performance. It feels like the skill is becoming more or less automatic with practice. Furthermore, just as skills take time to develop, they tend to be very durable. Unlike facts, you don't lose skills rapidly, even over long periods without practice. Although you can lose or "forget" a skill, this occurs far more slowly than forgetting facts.

So, with training, we acquire new facts and skills. As the saying goes, practice (with the experience it provides) makes perfect, and the more practice you put in, the more perfect your performance will be. A *performance* is the use of a practiced skill. When you perform, you put what you know into action. Some kinds of performance rely more heavily on facts (for example, reciting the states and their capitals), whereas others require an emphasis on skills (for example, playing the piano). Thus, the best way to train depends on the type of performance that you are training for. In this book, we explain which training techniques work best for different types of performance goals.

What age do you have to be to benefit from mental training? Any age! Although some skills, such as learning a second language, are easier to learn when you're a child, you can still learn a new activity at just about any age if you are willing to invest the effort. You can even become an expert at it. Gary Marcus, a psychology professor, made this point by becoming a guitar expert in his middle years even though he started out completely "tuneless."[1]

Training doesn't have to involve a new activity, though. The goal of your training might be to maintain or improve your skill at a current favorite activity. Maybe you've been a musician all your life, but you want to improve some aspect of your technique or expand your knowledge of certain composers. Mental training will help!

---

[1]You can read about Gary in his book: Marcus, G. (2012). *Guitar zero*. New York, NY: Penguin Group.

Thus, what you learn in this book can help you if you identify with any of the three following cases:

- *Case 1*. Suppose you are a young person. You're just starting out in adult life. Maybe you just got your first job. The question is, how good at that job do you want to be? Or, while working at it, are you looking around for your real calling? You have plenty of time and you want to be the very best you can be at whatever it is you'll be pursuing. Training can help you get there.
- *Case 2*. You are in middle age. You've been working at the same job for 20 years and have become pretty good at it, but you're looking to expand your horizons. You want to reinvigorate your life by adding something new. You don't have a lot of free time, but you can certainly add something to your life. Suppose all of a sudden you decide to learn to paint in watercolors. Can it be done, and at a level that keeps your interest? Training can help you get there.
- *Case 3*. You are retired. You've had a rich and challenging career, but now you're done doing what you've been doing all your life. You're ready to take on something new and different, if only to keep yourself mentally sharp or stable. Maybe you want to take on art history. Training can help you pick it up in a satisfying way. Hopefully, this training will allow you to retain your mental ability and reverse what might otherwise be a mental decline.

So go ahead and choose a goal for training. What do you want to get better at? What are you most interested in? Music, sports, medicine, accounting, the stock market, carpentry? Pick your activity and goal, commit to it, and let's begin.

WHAT WILL IT TAKE TO BECOME AN EXPERT?

Have you ever admired the performance of a top athlete, a highly skilled musician, or an appraiser on *Antiques Roadshow* and wondered how that person got to be so good? Have you ever dreamed of being that good at anything? Maybe you can be. Elite performance is not born but made. Here's the key: You have to work at it, and you have to really want it. In other words, you need time and effort, as well as motivation.

Time and Effort

Researchers have different estimates of how much time and effort are required to become an expert, and some areas of expertise are harder than others. Anders Ericsson, the leading researcher in this field who has studied the history of experts in many domains, concludes that it takes approximately 10,000 hours of deliberate study and practice to really master a task—that is, to become an expert. Deliberate practice is practice done consciously and intentionally, especially on aspects of the task that challenge your weaknesses. 10,000 hours! That's a lot of time. That's about 3 hours a day, every day of the year, for 10 years. The popular cartoon *Dilbert* has even joked about this amount (see Figure 1.1). Clearly, neither Dilbert's boss nor his interviewee is quite there yet!

Motivation

Although 10,000 hours may seem daunting, don't be discouraged. The following facts should boost your motivation:

- *Progress comes quickly.* The learning curve (which shows your progress over a series of practice sessions) is steep to begin with.

FIGURE 1.1. Dilbert's Boss and The Interviewee Both Need More Practice

Early practice has a bigger payoff than later practice. Look at the idealized learning curve in Figure 1.2. You will probably get to be pretty good at any new task after a month or so of deliberate and systematic practice. It might take years to become really, really good, but it doesn't take years to make progress.

- *Progress begets progress.* There is something called a *positive feedback loop* operating in most training situations. You can see your progress, especially if you keep reasonable evaluative records of how well you're doing. You can "see" your learning curve, and that information feeds positively into future performance. Figure 1.3 illustrates a positive feedback loop.
- *Progress leads to more commitment.* Performance improvement fuels commitment. Doing better at something is its own reward. It has the effect of encouraging more work and even better performance.

The point of all this is to motivate you to get started. Apply yourself, and watch what happens. Before you know it, deliberate

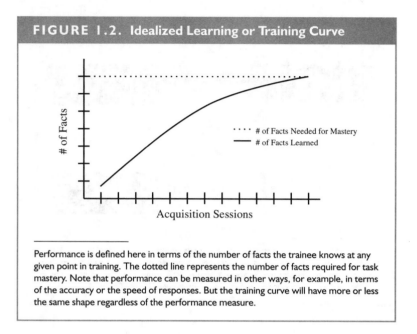

FIGURE 1.2. Idealized Learning or Training Curve

Performance is defined here in terms of the number of facts the trainee knows at any given point in training. The dotted line represents the number of facts required for task mastery. Note that performance can be measured in other ways, for example, in terms of the accuracy or the speed of responses. But the training curve will have more or less the same shape regardless of the performance measure.

practice will become a standard routine, and the whole process of acquiring knowledge and skills will become self-sustaining. You might even begin to look forward to practice sessions lasting 2 to 3 hours. Early on, the key is to "stick to it."

IS THERE AN EASIER PATH TO BETTER PERFORMANCE?

Do you really need to practice all that much? Can you get away without that effort? Can you influence your brain in some way to do the work for you? Let's consider some possibilities.

First, you might think that having great genes could eliminate at least some of your need for practice. Maybe you have always found mental activities easy. Could that be because of your native intelligence, which you inherited from your parents?

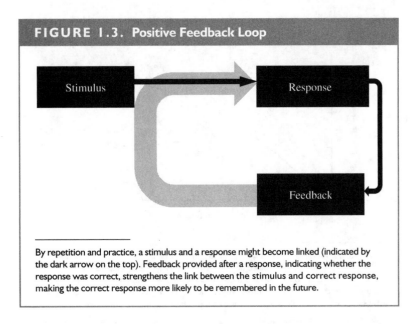

FIGURE 1.3. Positive Feedback Loop

By repetition and practice, a stimulus and a response might become linked (indicated by the dark arrow on the top). Feedback provided after a response, indicating whether the response was correct, strengthens the link between the stimulus and correct response, making the correct response more likely to be remembered in the future.

Maybe so, but the scientific evidence is not compelling. Further, even the smartest people need to practice in order to keep themselves mentally fit, just as the most talented musicians and athletes need to practice deliberately and frequently to stay at the top of their fields.

Second, you might think that you can take a pill that will keep you mentally fit. Many paid advertisements, such as the one in Media Clip 1.1, try to tell you this. Indeed, there are even some scientific studies suggesting that some widely marketed nonprescription drugs can serve as memory enhancers or can effectively treat the decline in memory due to aging. But a careful review of scientific studies suggests that the specific evidence is not yet strong enough to warrant buying those products as an easy way out of mental training.

Third, you might think that you can improve performance by changing your diet, being careful to eat the right foods and to get the

MEDIA CLIP 1.1.

Memory Pill Helps the Brain Like Prescription Glasses Help the Eyes, Claims US Surgeon General Candidate

Help is on the way for those who routinely lose their car keys, get lost while driving, forget to call people back, or misplace their TV remote control.

Just like a good pair of glasses can make blurry vision sharp and crystal-clear, there's a new, doctor-recommended memory pill that may help your brain, sharpening your memory and mental powers, and making that slow-thinking, sluggish brain as sharp as a tack . . .

Ad appeared in *The News Herald* on April 30, 2013. To see the full ad, go to http://ads.denverpost.com/ads/201550.

right vitamins and nutrients, and that such changes will relieve your need for mental training. For example, vitamin D, ginseng, caffeine, sugar, omega 3 oil, avocados, and berries have all been touted as food items that enhance memory, increase the ability to concentrate, and improve attention span. Our favorite "smart" or "brain" food of this type is chocolate! You should indeed try to eat a healthy diet, but this is not a panacea that will eliminate your need for mental training. Eating the right foods is necessary to keep your mind and your body active, alert, and functioning well, but it is not sufficient. You also have to train your mind.

Finally, you might think that physical exercise or bodybuilding can substitute for mental training. Some have argued that physical fitness is the cornerstone of mental fitness. Unfortunately, the "scientific" evidence cited to support this claim doesn't stand up under close scrutiny. Physical exercise is important for a happy and healthy adult life, but if you want to improve mentally, exercise your mental functions. There is really no easy route to high-level mental performance that does not entail mental work. As the saying goes, there's no free lunch. And mental work is hard, there's no getting around it. Jane Fonda often said in her fitness workout videos, "No pain, no gain." She's right, and that goes for mental exercise as much as it does for physical fitness and sports training. We discuss these possibilities here because we want to help you to identify what does and what does not work when it comes to improving your mind. Commit yourself to working hard, and you will see the benefits in the way you can do your daily activities.

DO YOU NEED A COACH?

For physical fitness training, it is often wise to get some help from someone knowledgeable and skilled in exercise techniques. A coach can give you a set of activities, showing you each exercise, watching you perform the exercise, and giving you feedback on your performance. The coach can select those exercises so that they are appropriate to your precise level of fitness, your level of skill, and the time you have to conduct your training. You then perform your exercises at home, perhaps every morning before breakfast. When you think that you have mastered those exercises, you can return to your coach for an assessment of your level of progress. Your coach will probably ask to see you do each exercise as a way to monitor your performance and then will give you tips to improve each exercise, change it, or take you to a higher level. The coach will also add some new exercises to give you some variety and keep you interested in your exercise program and motivated to continue with it.

What about mental training? There is no doubt that a coach can be helpful in guiding your mental training program the same way that a coach can be helpful in guiding your physical training program. So who can serve as a mental training coach? It depends on the area in which you've chosen to concentrate your mental training efforts. For example, if your chosen area of concentration involves music, try to find a music teacher. If your chosen area involves art, look for a professional artist or art educator. Likewise, if your chosen area is writing, then look for a professional writer. Finally, if your chosen area is an academic discipline, try to find a professor or graduate student teaching that discipline at a local college. These individuals might not have served in this precise way in the past; guiding a program of mental training in this area might be new to them. But they should be willing to help you in this way and should find it a stimulating and enjoyable experience to do this type of tutoring. They might be willing to help you on a volunteer basis. Alternatively, it might be appropriate to pay them for their time and effort. Coaches add value to a training program, but use them sparingly.

DO YOU NEED A TRAINING PARTNER?

Another possibility is to work with a training partner. If you and a friend or relative both want to start a mental training program, maybe you can help each other develop the training routine. Working alongside someone else can help you stick to that routine. You should meet regularly to discuss what your goals are and how you plan to achieve them. You can formulate exercises that you can each conduct individually at your own pace and on your own schedule, and then you can regularly check on each other's progress. Or you might decide to do the training together, perhaps alternating the exercises with conversation and coffee or a snack. Your mental training sessions can become a social occasion for you. They can give you the opportunity to spend some time with your friend in a new way and with a new focus. Naturally, this idea will work best if you both choose the same area in which to train. But if you choose different areas, perhaps both of you can train in both areas. Then you can serve as the leader in the area you chose, and your friend can serve as the leader in the other area.

Although it might be fun, motivating, and helpful to involve another individual, either as a coach or as a training partner, it is usually not necessary. Just as you don't need someone to help you find books to read for pleasure, you don't need someone to help you find mental exercises that you enjoy and promote training. Indeed, many people prefer to do all of the training on their own. Formulating your mental exercise program and then conducting the exercises can be your time for solitude. If you are a self-starter and want to find some time for yourself, then go for it!

HOW CAN YOU STAY FOCUSED?

Training is hard, sometimes boring, sometimes fatiguing. It requires sustained attention. Don't be surprised if, on occasion, your mind begins to wander during practice. It happens to most people. So you have to guard against it because your ability to stay on task contributes to your level of performance. Here are some tips that might help you.

First, keep your training sessions short; the longer they are, the more susceptible you are to losing track. There is a balancing act here. A session needs to be long enough to show progress in performance, but short enough to minimize task disengagement. You might have to experiment to see what works best for you.

Second, there are ways to mitigate boredom. We discuss later possible antidotes to boredom that you can introduce into a session to keep your mind focused.

Finally, you can actually train yourself to stay focused, or *mindful*. Mindfulness training has been demonstrated to reduce the occurrence of distracting thoughts during tests of general knowledge and of memory, especially among trainees who are prone to distraction. Mindfulness training consists mainly of focused-attention meditation, such as focusing on the breath or other sensory experiences (e.g., tasting a fruit). If your mind tends to wander, but you can't take a course on mindfulness, it might still be helpful for you to practice focused-attention meditation techniques.

SETTING UP AN EFFECTIVE TRAINING PROGRAM

Give some structure to your practice. Decide how much time you can commit each week and each day within the week. Then decide what times during those days you will practice. Spread your practice out as much as possible; it is better to practice 1 or 2 hours each day of the week than to cram it all into one day. Find ways to reward yourself for sticking to your schedule. That will be a big part of keeping your motivation high. Additionally, keep a record of how well you do on each practice session. In other words, provide yourself with periodic feedback about the accuracy of your performance, the types of errors you make, and the speed with which you execute the task correctly. We discuss this in more detail throughout the book.

Maximizing the Three Goals of Training

In a formal training program, there are three types of sessions: (1) *acquisition* sessions, which include exposure, experience, and drills on new material; (2) *retention* sessions, which include testing your memory of material that you learned previously; and (3) *transfer* sessions, which include testing for improvement on different but related material.

The three types of training sessions promote three somewhat different goals. All three add to your level of performance. A good training program should maximize all three of these goals:

- *Training efficiency.* Look for ways to acquire the new knowledge and skill in the shortest possible time. Some conditions of training will slow you down, and others will speed up the process. Usually, you want the latter. We discuss some exceptions later in the book.
- *Training durability.* Whatever it is you learn—new facts, a new skill—you want it to last, to stick with you. You need to be able to remember it, sometimes over long periods of time with little or no additional practice. Some training procedures support durable performance, others less so.
- *Training generalizability.* Sometimes training in one task will help you not only with that task, but also with related tasks. For example, say you learn to play a piece of music on the piano. Does that accomplishment transfer to other pieces of music so that you are better at pieces you have not practiced? Does your piano practice help you to play a different musical instrument? If either of these things happen, what you've

learned is to some degree *generalizable*. Although most new learning is quite specific, some training conditions promote transfer or generalizability.

So, by training, you want to optimize efficiency, durability, and generalizability of new knowledge and skill. It would be ideal if a training routine could optimize all three simultaneously, but life, unfortunately, is usually not that simple. What promotes efficiency of training does not necessarily enhance durability or generalizability. To take a simple example, making the training task easy will enhance speed of acquisition (efficiency), but often at a price in retention (durability). Things that are learned rapidly tend to be forgotten rapidly. Consider what happens when you "cram" the night before an exam. By cramming, it might seem that you saved study time. But what you "cram in" is often far less durable than it would be if you spread out the same amount of study time. "Crammed in" knowledge, lacking durability, is more likely to be forgotten after the exam.

Optimizing the three aspects of good training is something of a balancing act. For the math-oriented folks, it's like trying to solve three simultaneous equations for three unknowns. But don't despair. It can be done. In this book, we take a look at what works.

Planning the Training Sessions

Training takes place over days and weeks and maybe years, depending on your goal and your motivation. On any given day of training, you might work for, say, 1 to 3 hours on your routine. In the course of a given day, you might mix up acquisition with retention and transfer sessions. It's important to set them up and plan them in advance. You can do it alone, but this is where a coach might be helpful. The point is, training is a long process. It will consist of a variety of activities, all contributing to improved performance.

Measuring Success

Efficiency, durability, and generalizability are measured in different ways. Efficiency is gauged by how well you perform during the initial phase of training (the acquisition phase). You set a goal for the training session, and how quickly you get there tells you something about the efficiency of the acquisition process. Durability is measured in a follow-on retention phase. That is, after acquisition and the passage of a certain amount of time, you test performance for how much you've retained. Are you just as good as you were at the end of acquisition? Better maybe? Or have you lost something from the end of acquisition? This tells you about how durable the training experience was. Finally, how general is the training effect? Generality also is measured in a later test, after acquisition, in a transfer session. But now instead of measuring performance on the same material studied in acquisition, you measure it on new or related material. So let's say you learned 12 new facts in your chosen field during acquisition. We now test to see whether that new knowledge boosts what you know about other facts in the same general area. Or, alternatively, did the acquisition phase in any way affect how fast you can learn a new set of facts? If so, there is something general that you acquired in the initial phase. We will look at some real examples of these effects later on. It is vitally important to keep a written record of your performance in all three types of training sessions. These records provide the basis of enhanced performance via feedback through the positive feedback loop. And they will serve as a reminder of your improvement over time, keeping you motivated to continue.

We want to emphasize that training effects tend to be quite specific to the material—the facts and the skills—trained on. If you're training to be a pianist, an ice skater, an accountant, or a brain surgeon, what you acquire during training will be relatively limited to those domains. Don't expect training to make you a genius. You'll get increasingly better at the task at hand. But you'll pretty much be the same old person when it comes to anything else. That's why doing mental exercises can entertain you and keep you alert and even improve how well you can do *those* exercises. But they won't make you any smarter in general.

THE STOOL METAPHOR

It is useful to think of training as a three-legged stool of adjustable height. The effects of training are represented by the stool seat. The seat can be raised or lowered, representing the level at which you currently perform. Performance level is supported by the three legs of the stool: efficiency, durability, and generalizability. Figure 1.4 gives a diagrammatic picture of the stool metaphor, which we will refer to throughout the book.

THE TAKEAWAY

This book shows you how to train your mind and improve your performance. We emphasize the role of deliberate practice on tasks that you want to become good at. To improve performance on any task, you need new knowledge and new skills. You'll have to work many hours. But you can do it, just as others have before you.

As we have noted, there are three goals of training: efficiency, durability, and generalizability. The majority of this book focuses on these goals. In Chapter 2, we discuss how to promote training efficiency—that is, how to learn quickly. In Chapter 3, we discuss how to promote training durability—that is, how to retain what you learn. In Chapter 4, we discuss how to promote

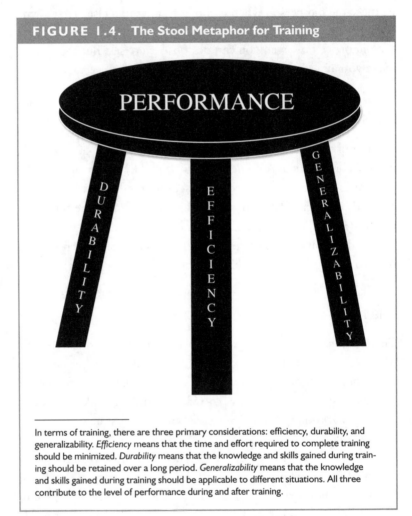

FIGURE 1.4. The Stool Metaphor for Training

PERFORMANCE

DURABILITY

EFFICIENCY

GENERALIZABILITY

In terms of training, there are three primary considerations: efficiency, durability, and generalizability. *Efficiency* means that the time and effort required to complete training should be minimized. *Durability* means that the knowledge and skills gained during training should be retained over a long period. *Generalizability* means that the knowledge and skills gained during training should be applicable to different situations. All three contribute to the level of performance during and after training.

training generalizability—that is, how to apply what you learn to new situations. Chapter 5 concludes the book by discussing some additional topics related to training, including how to refresh your skills, how aging affects your mental abilities, some common myths about training, and what's in the future for training.

Our training tips are all based on scientific evidence, although we do not review that evidence in depth.[2] Rather, we focus on simple training routines that help you learn the facts and skills you need to enhance performance in just about any task, job, or area you choose.

In addition to describing each training tip, we present an exercise for you to practice using that tip. Generally, it will take some practice for you to get used to each tip. But as you master each one, you should begin to see how that routine influences training effects. It is not enough merely to read a tip. You need to work on it, deliberately practice it! You are likely to find that some tips are more effective for you than others are. When that happens, take note of it. You will want to use the routines that are most effective for you.

The exercises we provide are often based on quite simple tasks. For example, we practice learning French vocabulary words even though speaking and understanding a foreign language involves much more than just knowing a few words. Our reasons for starting simple are twofold. First, most complex tasks can be broken down into simpler component tasks. Training on these simple component tasks, if done properly, can help you master the more complex whole task. So, learning vocabulary will play into the larger task of mastering the language. Second, you have to start somewhere. You'll find that learning the separate components of a complex task is a lot easier than

---

[2]The scientific research is described in depth in our research volume: Healy, A. F., & Bourne, L. E., Jr. (2012). *Training cognition: Efficiency, durability, and generalizability.* New York, NY: Psychology Press.

trying to master the whole thing at once. You'll show faster progress on a part task than on the whole task. Simplifying will pay off in time saved in the long run. Moreover, there is some evidence that there is greater transfer from simple tasks to hard tasks (or whole tasks) than there is from hard tasks to simple tasks (or part tasks). To us, this is another reason to start simple. The methods of training, however, are very much the same for simple and hard tasks. So you will be able to use the same training methods that we discuss in the text as you progress to more complex tasks.

CHAPTER 2

HOW TO LEARN QUICKLY: INCREASING THE EFFICIENCY OF TRAINING

The more intelligible a thing is, the more easily it is retained in the memory, and contrariwise, the less intelligible it is, the more easily we forget it.

—the Benedict Spinoza Doctrine

Training efficiency is one of the crucial legs of the training stool (see Chapter 1). For any given training session, you want to try to reach your goals as quickly and effortlessly as possible. But there is a need to be cautious here. As we note in Chapter 1, training quickly can have adverse effects on the other two crucial legs, durability and generalizability. Often, quick learning leads to quick forgetting. Quick learning can also lead to specific learning that doesn't generalize well. Thus, we want to use training routines that enhance efficiency without sacrificing durability and generalizability. We discuss this trade-off in greater depth later. In general, this chapter focuses on practical tips to increase your training efficiency.

GET THE RIGHT FEEDBACK AT THE RIGHT TIME

Be sure to get feedback during training based on the recorded performance measures you are using. Feedback is a measure of your progress. For example, if you are trying to learn typing, your feedback could be the number of words typed per minute (i.e., your typing speed) or the number of errors committed (i.e., your accuracy). Keep track of your progress as you go by writing down your score (for speed, accuracy, or both). Remember that according to the positive feedback loop discussed in Chapter 1, getting a little positive feedback will reinforce your motivation and improve your performance. Thus, it's good to monitor your progress.

What kind of feedback is useful? *Trial-by-trial feedback* (which is where you get feedback after every time you try the task) has been shown to help you learn, especially early in training. This might be because it motivates you to set increasingly higher standards of performance or because it identifies errors and shows how to correct them. Indeed, feedback is most effective when it serves to correct errors, and feedback might have little or no benefit after correct responses. But in some tasks, you will have a good sense anyway of how well you're doing without feedback. In those circumstances, trial-by-trial feedback might not be the best procedure and might actually be distracting, confusing, or interfering.

If trial-by-trial feedback is too distracting, try *periodic summary feedback*—that is, get feedback on only some portion of training trials, or get feedback on your average performance over time. In the typing example, this would be equivalent to testing your speed and accuracy only once per hour and monitoring your daily averages from one day to the next. Indeed, often the frequency of feedback given during acquisition can be gradually reduced without adverse effects. The idea is to get useful feedback, but not too much of it. Get feedback, but only as much as is helpful.

You can use what you know about the positive feedback loop and the learning curve (see Chapter 1) to facilitate the training process. In fact, it's a good idea to create a record of your performance after each training session so that you can see your improvement over time—that is, your *learning curve*. For those who like visual aids, you might even create a graph showing your performance over time. If you have a computer, use it to store records and to create graphic representations of your performance. The general trend in this learning curve should be upward, but don't get too concerned if you occasionally falter. The learning curve reflects the role of feedback in the training process and should help to maintain your level of motivation.

Try Exercise 2.1 to determine how much and when to get feedback to maximize your training efficiency. This exercise uses French vocabulary as the subject, but you can adjust the exercises in this book for any subject that you are working on. Other examples might be music composers and their compositions or brain structures and their primary functions.

MAKE SURE NEW MATERIAL IS NEITHER TOO DIFFICULT NOR TOO EASY

Each new acquisition session should add to something you've already learned. For example, if the focus is on fact learning, then you'll want to train on some number of new facts in each session. If you're working on a skill or a mental procedure, like the steps of CPR, then you'll need to move on to some higher (faster) level of performance. But how much should you add in each new session? Follow the Goldilocks rule: You don't want to add too little because that might make the new task trivial, but you also don't want to add too much because that might impede your progress. This in-between area (not too little, not too much) is called the *zone of learnability*.

The zone of learnability, or *zone of possible improvement*, refers to the region that is just a bit beyond what you can do at present. What you add should provide some challenge to you but not be overwhelming. If the additions are too easy, you won't be able to learn anything new from them because you have already mastered the required knowledge and skills. On the other hand, if the additions are too difficult, you won't be able to learn anything new from them because you do not have the prerequisite knowledge and skills.

EXERCISE 2.1. Feedback Effects in Fact Learning

Almost any kind of feedback, assuming it's accurate, will improve your performance. However, some types of feedback will improve your performance more than others. This exercise shows how feedback works in the training process. For this exercise, you will need sixty 3 × 5 cards with a French word and its English translation on one side of each card and the French word alone on the other side. If you already know French, replace French with another language that you'd like to learn.

Part 1: Periodic feedback. Divide the 60 cards into three 20-card decks. Shuffle the cards in each deck. Then start training by trying to learn the meaning of the first 20 words. Study them one at a time for 5 minutes.

Next, give yourself a quiz on the first five words. To do that, for each of the five French words occurring alone on one side of a card, write down what you think is its English equivalent, guessing if necessary. Now give yourself feedback on your success by turning the five cards over to see the answer and correcting your answer sheet as needed. How many did you get right? Now quiz yourself on the next five French words. After that quiz, give yourself feedback, and continue in that way until you have quizzed yourself on all 20 words, with feedback.

Now take a test on all 20 French words to see how effective this training regimen was for you. Score your test, and see how many of the words you got correct. That score will tell you how effective periodic feedback is for you.

Part 2: Immediate feedback. Now let's determine how effective immediate feedback (that is, trial-by-trial feedback) is for you. Turn to a second set of 20 French words and study them for 5 minutes.

Then quiz yourself on the 20 words, but this time look up your answer immediately after each guess. In other words, quiz yourself one French word at a time—write down your best guess for each word, and then immediately check the answer and give yourself feedback. When you are finished guessing and getting feedback on all 20 French words in this set, you are ready to take a test on all 20 words.

To take your test on all 20 words, look at each French word and write down the English translation. Do not check your answers until

EXERCISE 2.1. Feedback Effects in Fact Learning (*Continued*)

you've completed all 20 words. Then score your test, and see how many of the words you got correct. How did you do on the test this time? Did you do better on Part 2 with immediate (trial-by-trial) feedback or on Part 1 with periodic summary feedback?

Part 3: Delayed feedback. If you've done Parts 1 and 2, you have probably found that periodic feedback is better than immediate feedback. You might now wonder whether the feedback can be given even less frequently than after five trials. So this time, turn to the third set of 20 French words and study them for 5 minutes.

Instead of giving yourself a quiz on one word at a time (as in Part 2) or on five words at a time (as in Part 1), give yourself a quiz on all 20 words. Then check your answers, giving yourself delayed feedback.

Finally, take the test on this set of 20 French words. How did you do this time? Was delayed feedback better than immediate feedback or periodic feedback? Did you do best on Parts 1, 2, or 3?

Of course, your performance on the three tests will depend not only on the feedback schedule but also on other factors, such as the particular words in each set of 20 and how tired you are during each test. Also, your performance should probably improve as you go from one set of words to the next just because of the benefits of practice. So you might want to repeat the exercises another time in a different order and see if each time you get the same answer to the question of which feedback schedule is best for you.

In these exercises, you gave yourself only one quiz on each set of words before taking the test on those words. But if you really want to learn all the words perfectly, you will probably need to take more than one quiz. The question then arises whether all 20 words should be included in each quiz or whether instead you should use a "dropout" procedure, where you quiz yourself on only the words you missed the last time. So, for example, let's say on your first quiz you missed 10 words. Then limit the second quiz to just those words that you missed on the first

(continued)

EXERCISE 2.1. Feedback Effects in Fact Learning
(*Continued*)

quiz. Now see how many of those words you made errors on. Perhaps you made errors on only five words this time. So limit the third quiz to just those five words. You can continue quizzing yourself using this dropout procedure until you make no more errors. Then give yourself the final test. You should do very well on the test this time, even if you don't get a perfect score. The dropout procedure can be very effective and efficient, suggesting that practice on words you already know isn't always a good use of your limited time!

How can you determine your zone of learnability? Check your learning curve, as illustrated in Figure 2.1. Keep good performance records. Use the records to create a session-by-session representation of performance, showing where you are at the beginning of the current training session (or where you were at the end of the last). You can use graph paper to chart the learning curve or a computer if you have the know-how. It might take a little experimenting on your part, but let's guess, intuitively, that in the next session you can add about 10% new facts to be learned or can increase your speed by 10%. On the basis of your learning curve, you want to set your additions for the next acquisition session to be above, but not too far above, the height of your learning curve (your current level of performance). Here's one way to do it, using French vocabulary learning as an example. Of course, you can substitute another language for French to get the same practice.

Start by picking 20 words in French (or another language that you are trying to learn) and determining their English translations. Study the French–English word pairs for 5 minutes. Then test yourself on the word pairs. How many did you get right? Let's say you got 10 pairs correct. In the next session, you might want to restudy

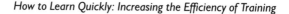

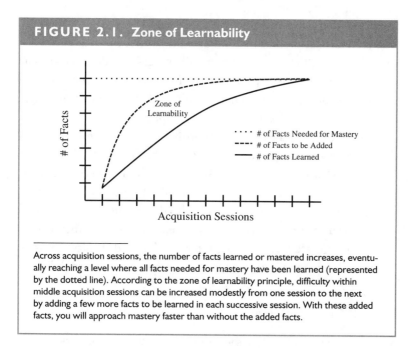

FIGURE 2.1. Zone of Learnability

Across acquisition sessions, the number of facts learned or mastered increases, eventually reaching a level where all facts needed for mastery have been learned (represented by the dotted line). According to the zone of learnability principle, difficulty within middle acquisition sessions can be increased modestly from one session to the next by adding a few more facts to be learned in each successive session. With these added facts, you will approach mastery faster than without the added facts.

the 10 correct pairs but add in some of the incorrect pairs, choosing the number to add within your zone of learnability. For example, try adding in three pairs, remembering that the eventual goal is to master all 20 pairs. If you now get all 13 (10 old and three new) correct, your zone of learnability is at least three pairs. In the next session try adding in four more pairs. If you are able to get all of the pairs correct (10 oldest, three older, four new), then your zone of learnability is at least four pairs. But if you fail to get all of the pairs when you've added four, you have probably exceeded your zone of learnability. An exercise like this one will help you establish the best number of pairs for you to add on each succeeding acquisition session. Note that this training method, based on the zone of learnability, differs from the dropout method discussed in Exercise 2.1 because mastered items are restudied in the zone-of-learnability method. The zone-of-learnability method and the dropout method are both reasonable, but they have different advantages and drawbacks. The dropout method is clearly more efficient, but it might not be optimal in terms of durability or generalizability. Thus, there is no single method that should be used in every training situation.

The zone of learnability will probably not be constant. It will depend on how alert you are or how easy the tasks are. Also, as you practice, you will probably increase your zone of learnability. And as you get tired or fatigued, your zone will probably decrease. For different training exercises, your zone will also differ. But now you should see how you can constantly adjust your exercises so that they will be at the appropriate level for you in terms of their difficulty. Exercise 2.2 gives you more practice determining your zone of learnability.

PRACTICE IN YOUR HEAD

Sometimes you are not in the right environment to practice. You have the time, but you may not have the right materials or equipment at hand. Think of a pianist without a piano. Maybe you're a downhill skier preparing for a slalom, but presently you're sitting in your living room, not at the ski slopes. How about in training as an emergency technician—can you run through the steps of CPR in your head? You can pretty much always imagine yourself in the right context. To practice mentally, you have to be able to visualize or "feel" the action you're trying to perfect. If you have the page of music in front of you, you won't have to visualize the musical notes, but you will need to picture your instrument in your mind's eye, execute in a virtual way the finger actions prescribed by the musical line, and "hear" the sound created by each keystroke. The more faithfully you can perform these tasks, the more useful the practice will be. Like most other activities we've discussed, mental practice

---

EXERCISE 2.2. The Zone of Learnability

This exercise is pretty straightforward. It shows that, for efficient learning, new material should be added to what you already know in measured amounts—not too much, not too little. First, choose two sets of 20 French words (for a total of 40 words) and their English translations. You will use one set for Part 1 below and another set for Part 2. If French isn't your subject, you can choose another language or just use facts from whatever subject you are trying to master.

Part 1: From the first set of 20 words, study 10 words until you can translate them all correctly—that is, until you can provide the correct English translation for each French word. How many times did you have to repeat the list in order to get all 10 words correct?

Add in the remaining 10 words, and determine how many list repetitions are required to get all 20 words in the set correct. Rest a bit.

Part 2: From the second set of 20 words, study and practice 10 words until you can do them all correctly. The number of list repetitions needed should be pretty much the same as for the first 10 words in Part 1 if the words are equally difficult. But now the procedure changes.

Add in five of the remaining words, and practice until you can get all 15 words correct. After that, add in the remaining five words, and practice until you can get all 20 words correct. If your zone of learnability is closer to five than 10 for French vocabulary words, you should find that the second procedure requires fewer total repetitions than the first to master the entire list of 20 words. Once you know your zone of learnability, you can use that information to plan your acquisition training sessions.

---

is a learnable skill. The more you practice doing it, the better you'll become. You'll find it a handy skill to acquire to promote training efficiency in any task.

Is it of any value to practice mentally? Not always, but often it is. Thus, it's worth trying. What do you have to lose? Mental practice won't take the place of physical practice, but it can still help. In fact, cognitive psychological studies have shown that under some circumstances, mental practice can be even better than physical practice. In one study, mental practice was better than physical practice when the physical practice was restricted and had to be executed with the wrong limbs (for example, with the left hand as opposed to the preferred right hand). Let's say you need to practice a new cursive writing style, but you have hurt your writing hand. You could practice the writing style with your other hand, or you could mentally practice with your writing hand. Which would be better? The results of the laboratory experiments imply that you might benefit more from mental practice with the correct hand than physical practice with the wrong hand.

Mental practice can be done in various ways, and they are not all equally effective. The *first-person* way involves imagining yourself doing the practice. The *third-person* way involves imagining another person doing the practice. Generally, first-person mental practice is more effective than third-person mental practice, but sometimes the latter can still improve your performance. In fact, instead of imagining other individuals practicing, you can sometimes actually observe others practice. Learning by observation of another can be quite helpful, which is why instructional videos are so popular. By watching someone else do the practice, you can see at least one effective way that the practice can be done and perhaps spot differences between your performance and someone else's, which might eliminate errors on your part if the other person actually performs better. Exercise 2.3 demonstrates the effectiveness of mental practice.

AS TRAINING PROGRESSES, CHANGE YOUR FOCUS OF ATTENTION

No matter how skilled you are at a task, there will always be something new to be learned. Developing expertise in any area is always a work in progress. In competitive sports, there will be things to find

---

EXERCISE 2.3. Mental Practice

Mental practice is especially useful for learning skills (as opposed to facts). Let's say that the activity you're trying to master is playing the clarinet. Will mental practice work for you? To answer that question, try practicing both ways, physically and mentally.

Get out your music and your clarinet, and practice playing a song on the clarinet for 10 minutes. Now mentally practice a second song for the same length of time. Basically, this amounts to thinking through your fingering while reading the music but without your instrument. Then test yourself on the two songs, and see how well you do on each of them. Count how many times you made errors or had to start the song over. Did you do as well on the second song as on the first?

Of course, the two songs might not have been equivalent for some reason. So this short test would not be definitive unless you repeat it with a variety of songs, alternating between mental and physical practice for the songs. If you do as well with mental practice as with physical practice, then you know that mental practice is a viable strategy for you to use. In actual training, physical practice and mental practice are often combined, with mental practice being used whenever physical practice is not possible (for example, whenever your clarinet is unavailable).

---

out about your next opponent. In piano playing, there will be unfamiliar pieces. Your next encounter, then, will require you to focus your attention on certain new aspects of the task at hand. Where you focus your attention has an important impact on your success.

There are two general ways that you can focus your attention in sports, in music, and in any other skill. You might focus *internally* on various parts of your body that are involved in performance. Alternatively, you might focus *externally* on the results of your movements, as illustrated in Figure 2.2. If you're learning to dance, you can focus on where to put your feet (internal) or on coordinating your actions with those of your partner (external). Consider a simpler example,

---

FIGURE 2.2. Focus of Attention

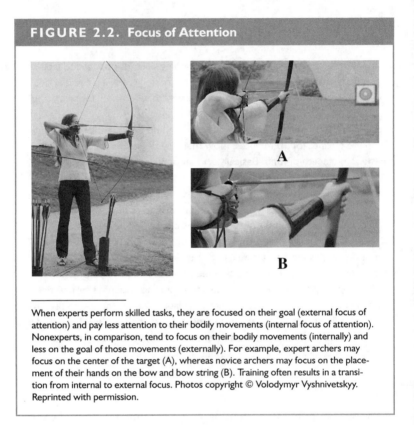

When experts perform skilled tasks, they are focused on their goal (external focus of attention) and pay less attention to their bodily movements (internal focus of attention). Nonexperts, in comparison, tend to focus on their bodily movements (internally) and less on the goal of those movements (externally). For example, expert archers may focus on the center of the target (A), whereas novice archers may focus on the placement of their hands on the bow and bow string (B). Training often results in a transition from internal to external focus. Photos copyright © Volodymyr Vyshnivetskyy. Reprinted with permission.

---

throwing darts at a dartboard. You can focus your attention either on your arm and wrist movements or on the flight of the dart and its landing location relative to the bulls-eye on the dartboard.

Is either type of focus more effective for training in a new situation or task? More often than not, an external focus leads to higher levels of performance than an internal focus, and this result holds for a variety of activities. Why is this so? It seems that an internal focus, but not an external focus, requires conscious attention to specific movements. When your skill is well developed, many of these movements happen almost automatically and don't require your full attention. In fact, paying attention to highly skilled movements slows them down and thus impairs your performance. So, if you are moderately good at golf or dancing, you are likely to perform better if you concentrate on the golf ball or on your dance partner than if you try to control the individual components of your swing or your body movements. Ask professional golfer Greg Norman, who blew a seven-stroke lead in a Masters Golf Tournament. As he described it, he started thinking too much, focusing on each individual body movement involved in his swing. To put it simply, he "choked up." If you are already a pretty good golfer, then "just do it." Check out the difference between external and internal focus in Exercise 2.4.

EXERCISE 2.4. Varying Your Focus of Attention

Can you control your focus of attention? Can you concentrate on one thing while ignoring something else? Let's see, and then you can use that knowledge to benefit your training.

Let's start with a simple motor skill, like jump roping. This is something you're likely to be familiar with and can do at some level already. Get out your jump rope and practice for a few minutes. Now let's see if you can improve your jumping ability by changing your focus of attention. First, try an internal focus, during which you pay attention to your arm movements and the movements of your legs. How straight are your arms when you jump rope? How much do you bend your legs when you're jumping? Did you find that answering these questions made it easier or harder for you to jump rope? Probably consciously thinking of your arm and leg movements disrupts your jumping, at least mildly. Now try an external focus, during which you pay attention to the movement of the rope. How far away is the rope from your body when you are jumping? How far away is the rope from the ground as you jump over it? Did you find that answering those questions made it easier or harder for you to

(continued)

EXERCISE 2.4. Varying Your Focus of Attention (*Continued*)

jump rope? In this case, probably the questions did not disrupt your movements but maybe even allowed you to jump faster or longer.

Now try a simple perceptual-motor skill. Try to draw a perfect circle about 4 inches in diameter on a piece of paper. Draw 10 such circles, and see how good you can get at this skill. Now practice with an internal focus of attention, paying attention to your finger and hand movements by answering these questions to yourself as you draw 10 more circles: What is the best position for your fingers? How far away should your hand be from the paper? Okay, now draw 10 more circles, this time focusing externally on the shapes you are drawing rather than on the movements you are making by answering these questions to yourself as you draw the circles: Are the circles perfectly round, or are they oblong? How smooth is the line you draw for the circle?

Now look at and measure the diameter of the 10 circles you drew in each case. Are they closer to optimal (4 inches wide) for the external focus than for the internal focus? If so, the difference might be because you practiced with an external focus after you practiced with an internal focus. To rule out practice as a factor, a second session might be needed in which you practice with an external focus before you practice with an internal focus. Did the external focus still yield better circles? If so, you can see that an external focus is something you should try to achieve while learning a new skill or trying to improve a familiar one. The ability to focus your attention and to switch focus from one thing to another is itself a skill. The more you do it, the better you'll get at it. That skill turns out to be useful in a variety of task domains or jobs.

REST TO SPACE OUT YOUR PRACTICE

The way we've portrayed it so far, training consists mostly of hard work—study and test, study and test, rote learning. Sheer drudgery! If there's any fun to be had, it's far from obvious. You have to see increasingly better performance to keep your spirits up. But wait, there is evidence that rest between practice sessions can itself improve performance. By rest, we don't necessarily mean sleep. Rest can be any activity that turns your attention to other things besides training. Surprisingly, your performance is often boosted after you rest. The beneficial effect of rest seems to be that it lessens fatigue, disengagement, or inhibitions that might build up over prolonged practice. Another possibility is that during rest, you continue to think about the material just practiced. You begin to see the material in a new or different light and make connections within the material that you might have missed during practice. In other words, when you rest, you might be integrating what you learned during training. So, what's the bottom line? Don't think of rest as wasted time. It can have its own unique and beneficial effects. Consider taking time off from training, especially when your progress is slow. You might see a new side to the training process.

Let's say you plan to invest 3 hours a day in your training effort. You don't have to cram all your practice into a single sitting. In fact, it often works better to take some time away from practice. You could, for example, work an hour in the morning, another in the afternoon, and still another in the evening. It's really a question of convenience and your preferred study habits.

But here's an interesting twist. There is research to suggest that practice with rests is efficient for skill learning but not necessarily for fact leaning. Rests presumably help counteract motor fatigue, among other things, which is a benefit when your training has a motor component. In contrast, periodic rests might slow down learning new factual information because of the opportunity they provide for forgetting. So use rests judiciously, keeping in mind what you're trying to accomplish as an ultimate goal. Try Exercise 2.5 to get a sense of the benefits that rest can provide for training efficiency.

One thing you might try related to resting is called *expanding rehearsal.* Instead of keeping a consistent rest period between training sessions, try increasing this period gradually. For example, if

EXERCISE 2.5. Does Rest Really Help? See for Yourself

Let's say that you are training for two sets of tasks: one involving skill learning and the other involving fact learning. For the skill, maybe you are trying to improve your typing. To practice this skill, you might want to copy passages of a text, typing them into your computer. (Be sure to disable the auto-correct feature on your computer for any typing exercise.) Get a book and copy a passage from it for 5 minutes at a time, taking a 1-minute break between typing episodes. Don't do anything during the 1-minute break except relax. After you've typed for five 5-minute periods, have the computer count the number of words you typed. Also, check your typing to see how many errors you made. Now move to another part of the book, typing for 25 minutes solid, with no breaks. Again, see how many words you typed and how many errors you made. We bet that you did better with the breaks than without them. Were we right? If so, inserting rest breaks should help you learn a skill. Although you might think of rest periods as wasted time, you can usually use them to work on something else instead of just relaxing. So rest is better than no rest.

Now let's try the same type of exercise but for fact learning instead of skill learning. What kind of facts do you want to learn? Perhaps you'd like to memorize the telephone numbers of your friends and relatives. In that case, make a list of your friends and relatives, and beside each name put down the corresponding phone number. Be sure that the list is long, say 30 names. Study the first five name–number combinations for 5 minutes, and then take a 1-minute break. Then study the next five name–number combinations for 5 minutes, followed by another 1-minute break. Continue in this manner until you've studied the first 15 name–number combinations. Now test yourself. See how many of the telephone numbers you can list for the first 15 names. Also, time yourself on this task to see how long it takes you to fill in all of the phone numbers for the 15 names. After that test is over, study the next 15 name–number combinations for 15 minutes solid, with no breaks. And then test yourself on those names. Did you do better for the first set of 15 names or for the second set? Were you faster at responding for the first set of 15 names or for the second set?

EXERCISE 2.5. Does Rest Really Help? See for Yourself (Continued)

We bet that there wasn't much of a difference between the two sets. Rest breaks between trials probably don't help you when you are learning facts. There is a lesson to be learned here. Some study conditions will work better for fact learning, whereas others facilitate skill learning. Fortunately, we know a fair amount about what conditions work for what training goals. Using rest periods to space out your training is a powerful way to learn a skill.

you are taking four breaks, you might want to start with a break of 1 minute, then move to a break of 2 minutes, then switch to a break of 3 minutes, and end with a break of 4 minutes. These changes in rest times sometimes have a positive effect on training efficiency.

ADD A SIMPLE MENTAL TASK TO MINIMIZE BOREDOM

Suppose you're trying to improve your manual skills, for example, in typing or in entering data on the computer. Working too long on a boring task like this often worsens your performance rather than improves it. To get faster at a task, you sometimes trade off a decrease in accuracy in order to get an increase in speed. The deterioration in accuracy might be due to fatigue or boredom on your part. To witness a speed–accuracy trade-off in your own performance, do Exercise 2.6.

In some cases, you can counteract boredom and fatigue by adding a mental task to the training routine. For example, suppose you are training to enter four-digit numbers into a computer for a job. You could add a mental task by making a simple computation before entering each number. Maybe the computation is to decide whether the first two digits are smaller or larger than the second

---

EXERCISE 2.6. Speed Versus Accuracy

Sometimes, you might decide to let yourself make some errors in order to get a task done faster. But what about the opposite? Can you lower your speed to increase your accuracy? Yes, of course! If it is important for you to be accurate, then slow down your work and your accuracy will improve. Here's an exercise to show that such a trade-off is possible.

Let's consider again the task of typing. (And again, be sure to disable your computer's auto-correct feature.) Get another book, and record the time. Now, type a page from your book as quickly as you can. As soon as you finish, check the time. See how long it took you to type the page. Now, go back and proofread what you've typed. How many errors did you make? Next, record the current time and type the next page (assuming it is just as long as the first page), but this time type it as carefully as you can, trying to avoid errors. Again, as soon as you finish, check the time. It should have taken you more time to type the second page than the first. But what about the number of errors? Proofread your typing of the second page and see how many errors you made. This time you should have made fewer errors. If so, you have traded speed for accuracy. Now you see that you are in control of your speed–accuracy trade-off. But you should also realize that usually you can't have it both ways. A gain in one measure of performance will entail a loss in another. You can decide just how accurate you want to be. The cost of accuracy for you is just a slowing down in your speed. But if speed is more important to you than accuracy, you can adopt the opposite strategy.

---

two digits. Or maybe the added mental task is to add an alternating keystroke after each number, alternating between the plus key and the minus key. This simple added task, which doesn't take much time and might seem totally irrelevant, can serve as a "cognitive antidote" to boredom by having the positive effect of keeping you alert and thereby eliminating the speed–accuracy trade-off. It may even improve your performance during sessions of prolonged work.

BREAK TASKS INTO MANAGEABLE PARTS

Some tasks are too complicated to master all at once. It might help to break them into parts and practice each part separately first. This procedure should help to reduce the need for sharing attention between the parts (akin to multitasking), which can be a burden in the early going. We used that idea in preparing many of the exercises in this text. For example, a complex piece of music might be broken into different phrases and intensive practice given on each phrase in turn, before they are joined in a longer sequence. Alternatively, two parts that are normally performed concurrently, as with the left and right hands in a piano piece, might be practiced separately before trying to put them together. There is often a benefit to efficiency of training from this two-step procedure of training parts followed by training the whole.

Part training can also be based on part difficulty. This is sometimes called the "training wheels" approach. When you were a kid, you probably used training wheels before you rode a regular bike. Those training wheels made it a lot easier for you to keep your balance. When you had ridden the bike with training wheels for a while, you or your parents decided you were ready to move on to a regular bike. When you tried it at that point, you might have felt a little imbalanced, but your training-wheels practice probably helped you to master regular bike riding. The training-wheels experience was just what you needed to get you going!

A training-wheels approach can also help you learn other skills. The idea is to minimize errors by beginning training with the easiest items. As you master easy items, add more difficult items into the mix. The result is often a shorter time to learn the whole task. For example, maybe the skill you want to improve is your golf putting. That is a complex skill that requires precise hand–eye coordination. You might start practicing to make putts with the ball at very short distances from the hole. The very close distance is analogous to putting "with training wheels" because the short putt makes it easy to succeed. When you have mastered a short putt, move on to a putt at a longer distance, and continue to gradually increase the distance from the ball to the hole. By the end of this type of practice, you might find that you can get the ball into the hole with success and regularity at any distance!

But such part-task training methods don't work for every task. Sometimes breaking down a task into parts changes the overall task in ways that are not helpful. A task that is an integrated whole can be distorted if its parts are no longer interacting in their usual way. Thus, if the task for which you are training involves interlocking, or interdependent, parts—as is typical of many complex motor skills— it might not be best to use this part-task training strategy. Operating industrial machinery or driving an automobile are examples of tasks that require integrated coordination of an ensemble of interdependent actions and are probably best practiced in whole-task format.

How can we know whether part training will work for a given task? If the task contains parts that are performed in sequence (such as administering CPR), part training works best when you train the final segment first. In contrast, when the task contains parts that are performed simultaneously (such as skiing the slalom or swimming the breaststroke), part training might disrupt performance and probably should be avoided.

THE TAKEAWAY

We started this chapter with a quotation from Spinoza. It alludes to the fact that as you acquire new facts and skills through training, the material you study will become increasingly more meaningful to you. It stands to reason, then, that if these facts are meaningful to you at the outset, they will be acquired more efficiently. You will see repeated examples of this phenomenon, sometimes called the *Spinoza doctrine,* in the following chapters of this book. The training procedures we've just outlined can further enhance training efficiency, often with little cost in time and effort, and should be considered for any training program. They can be used to facilitate your development of expertise in your chosen area. Expertise development can be arduously slow at times, but like most things of value, getting there will be well worth the effort. Keep in mind, however, that, as we've said before, expertise is always a work in progress.

Table 2.1 summarizes the principles for learning quickly—that is, maximizing training efficiency. However, be aware that some valuable training techniques actually slow the training process down. That is, they operate in an *inefficient* fashion. If they slow down training, what then makes them valuable? At least some of them have a longer term payoff. Some of them enhance durability (or generalizability), thus offsetting the efficiency loss. So, let's discuss these procedures in the next chapter under the heading of *durability*.

TABLE 2.1. Training Principles for Efficiency: How to Learn Quickly

Purpose: Minimizing time and effort to achieve a training goal

Principle	Application
Feedback	Get the right feedback at the right time.
Zone of learnability	Make sure new material is neither too difficult nor too easy.
Mental practice	Practice in your head.
Focus of attention	As training progresses, change your focus of attention.
Spacing	Rest to space out your practice.
Cognitive antidote	Add a simple mental task to minimize boredom.
Part-task training	Break tasks into manageable parts.

CHAPTER 3

HOW TO RETAIN WHAT YOU LEARN: INCREASING THE DURABILITY OF TRAINING

My memory is so bad that many times I forget my own name.

—Miguel de Cervantes

Chapter 2 outlined what we know about promoting efficiency of training and what training efficiency will help you gain. We now turn our attention to the second stool leg, *durability of training,* which is the ability to retain what you learn (that is, to hold it in memory). Many folks complain about how bad their memory is, that what they've learned or experienced doesn't stick with them, isn't durable, isn't well retained. We hope that, unlike de Cervantes (author of the adventures of *Don Quixote*), you are not among them. But even if you are, improving memory is not as hard as it might seem. We don't have a magic formula that will, once and for all, make you a memory expert. But we do have recommendations for training that should, at the very least, give you a leg up on what you need to remember in order to do well in a specific area. There are two types of conditions that help you retain the facts and skills that you learn. One type will cause you to learn more slowly—that is, it lessens the efficiency of your training—whereas the other type will not. We discuss these conditions in separate sections of this chapter.

CONDITIONS THAT SLOW DOWN YOUR LEARNING

It is commonly accepted among trainers that the acquisition of new material should be made as easy as possible. Indeed, the part-training approach (see Chapter 2) requires that you start out with the easy stuff and then add to it. This approach works to some degree and in some cases. But there are also ways of enhancing the overall performance by making your training a little difficult—that is, by slowing down training. These conditions are sometimes referred to as *desirable difficulties,* for the obvious reason that they benefit later performance. Desirable difficulties are those acquisition difficulties that cause you to remember what you learn longer. Following are some ways to slow down your learning and remember the material longer.

As we discussed in Chapter 1, there are three types of training sessions: (1) *acquisition* sessions, which include practice on new material; (2) *retention* sessions, which include tests of your memory for that material; and (3) *transfer* sessions, which include tests on different but related material. To determine how well you retain what you learn, we look at your performance in the retention sessions. Remember, a retention session occurs after acquiring the material following some delay with no intervening practice.

Add Complications to the Training Task

If you make the training task difficult in some way, you slow down acquisition. There are lots of ways of doing that, and many, but not all, have a long-term benefit or are desirable. Here are some examples that are beneficial.

Let's say you're trying to learn a foreign language. Part of the task will be to build up a vocabulary of foreign words. You need to learn, let's say, the French equivalent of English words. Starting from scratch, you can present yourself with flash cards, showing the English–French pairs on one side and either the English word or the French word alone on the other. You study some pairs. Then you test yourself on either the English or the French member of each pair alone. Which of these tests is better for acquisition—testing for the French equivalent of English words or testing for the English equivalent of French words? Same question for retention. Presenting the French word and testing for the English is a lot easier than presenting the English word and testing for the French. So you will appear to acquire the French vocabulary a lot faster (more efficiently) in the French-to-English direction. But it's not enough to be able to translate French into English. In order to communicate in French, you must also be able to translate English to French. Learning in the English-to-French direction, although a lot harder and slower, will result in better retention of French–English pairings later and produce more fluency in general.

Another way to slow down your learning to increase your retention is to add interference to the items you learn during acquisition training. For example, in vocabulary learning, you can mix material across categories, like colors or parts of the body or names of trees, rather than group the material by category. This may slow down your initial acquisition, but it should help you remember the words better in the long run. This approach differs from the common "blocked practice" approach, which is to study each category separately. Although the blocked practice approach helps you learn material more quickly, it does not help you retain what you learn. Thus, if your goal is to remember material, the best approach might be to mix different types of material when you train. To see the differences between blocking and mixing practice, try Exercise 3.1.

So, when trying to master a large collection of new facts, start out by organizing them by category. Then before study, mix the facts up so that those from the same category are spread throughout

EXERCISE 3.1. Blocking or Mixing, Which Is Better?

Here's an exercise that can help you determine whether blocking or mixing tasks is better for learning a new skill. Do you know how to play the harmonica? Did you ever want to learn how to play some songs on it? Harmonicas are small, and you can probably carry one around wherever you go. Wouldn't it be great if you could play it well! The key, as with all training, is practice. One way to start practicing would be to learn to play four simple tunes on the harmonica. How about "Twinkle, Twinkle Little Star," "Row, Row, Row Your Boat," "Frère Jacques (Are You Sleeping?)," and "Happy Birthday to You." If you can play these four tunes well, then you can move on to more difficult tunes. The question is: How should you practice the simple tunes? Should you block practice, so you learn one song at a time? Or should you instead mix practice of the various tunes?

Let's divide the songs into two groups of two and try blocked practice for one group and mixed for the other. Then we can see which type of practice is best. Let's start with "Twinkle, Twinkle Little Star." Look up the notes for it on the Internet and practice it on the harmonica 10 times. After the 10 times, you should be pretty good at playing it! Now let's move on to the next song, "Row, Row, Row Your Boat." Find the notes for that tune, and practice playing it 10 times on the harmonica. Okay, you learned those two songs by blocked practice. How well did you learn the tunes? Test yourself by playing each tune again, and see how many mistakes you make and how seamlessly you can play each tune.

Now let's try mixed practice for the next two tunes. Look up the notes for the tunes "Frère Jacques" and "Happy Birthday to You." Instead of practicing one at a time, mix the practice of the two tunes, playing one and then the next, repeatedly across 10 repetitions each. Now test yourself on those two tunes. How well did you learn these two? See how many mistakes you make and how rapidly you can play these tunes.

Did you perform better following blocked practice or mixed practice? That is, did you make fewer errors on, and play more competently, the first two tunes or the second two tunes? Blocking is usually best for immediate tests like this one. So you should perform better on the first two tunes than on the second two tunes. But now let's see what

EXERCISE 3.1. Blocking or Mixing, Which Is Better? (Continued)

happens after a delay. Come back tomorrow or even a week later and test yourself again on all four tunes. Which tunes can you play most fluently, the fastest, and with the fewest errors? Mixing is usually best for delayed tests. So now you should perform better on the second two tunes than on the first two tunes. If you showed this expected pattern, then you will have demonstrated that blocking helps initial acquisition but mixing helps long-term retention.

However, as a miniexperiment, there is something wrong with this exercise. We've encountered this problem in other exercises. Blocking occurred before mixing, and whichever way you learn the songs, those practiced later would probably benefit from the prior experience with those practiced earlier. So you really need to repeat this exercise again, this time with mixing before blocking. So choose four more tunes— maybe simple holiday songs like Christmas carols this time—and repeat the exercise with the mixed practice preceding the blocked practice. Did you get the same results? Was blocking better for the immediate test and mixing better for the delayed test of these new tunes? Even if you didn't get this expected result, at least this exercise should make it clear to you what are the two types of practice, and you should be able to see which type you prefer.

This exercise and the blocking/mixing variable are quite flexible. If playing the harmonica is not your thing, see if you can find a comparable set of activities in your chosen task (e.g., different strokes in tennis). Moreover, blocking and mixing are not limited to just starting out on the task. You can block and mix subtasks at any stage of the game, including after you've become quite proficient. The effects of this variation in practice format should be pretty much the same no matter what is your level of skill.

a session. You'll slow down training somewhat, but you'll show a great gain in later retention of all facts.

Follow the Procedures Used by Memory Experts

You've probably heard of memory experts, sometimes called *mnemonists* or *memorists*. Memory experts seem to remember everything, without any effort. Of course, that's far from the truth. There is always a great deal of effort involved in trying to learn and remember things, even though some people are clearly better at it than others.

Some astounding feats of memory have been reported over the years. Numerous case histories of memory experts have been written and some fairly consistent patterns have been uncovered. Illustrative of these reports is the case of Rajan Mahadevan, who committed to memory the first 50,000 digits of the expansion of pi (see Figure 3.1). Rajan could recite the digits forward or backward or start anywhere in the middle, without hesitation or error. According to his report, he represented the expansion of pi in the form of 10×10 matrices and then used location within the given matrix as a cue to the digit that belonged in that location. This retrieval strategy seems too complex for most people to use. However, there is a lesson to be learned from Rajan's performance: to remember a new sequence of digits, some sort of special mental representation must be created.

Rajan's memory for numbers extended beyond pi and permitted him to listen to and repeat back quite long lists of random digits that were read to him. Memorizing new material took time and effort, but he was able to improve his memorizing speed by highly focused practice. Interestingly, his superior memory did not extend to all material, being only somewhat above the normal for letter strings and normal or worse on other material. Did he learn how to do this, or is it a gift or a fluke?

FIGURE 3.1. π = 3.14159 . . .

. . . 26535 89793 23846 26433 83279 50288 41971 69399 37510 58209 74944
59230 78164 06286 20899 86280 34825 34211 70679 82148 08651 32823 06647
09384 46095 50582 23172 53594 08128 48111 74502 84102 70193 85211 05559
64462 29489 54930 38196 44288 10975 66593 34461 28475 64823 37867 83165
27120 19091 45648 56692 34603 48610 45432 66482 13393 60726 02491 41273
72458 70066 06315 58817 48815 20920 96282 92540 91715 36436 78925 90360
01133 05305 48820 46652 13841 46951 94151 16094 33057 27036 57595 91953
09218 61173 81932 61179 31051 18548 07446 23799 62749 56735 18857 52724
89122 79381 83011 94912 98336 73362 44065 66430 86021 39494 63952 24737
19070 21798 60943 70277 05392 17176 29317 67523 84674 81846 76694 05132
00056 81271 45263 56082 77857 71342 75778 96091 73637 17872 14684 40901
22495 34301 46549 58537 10507 92279 68925 89235 42019 95611 21290 21960
86403 44181 59813 62977 47713 09960 51870 72113 49999 99837 29780 49951
05973 17328 16096 31859 50244 59455 34690 83026 42522 30825 33446 85035
26193 11881 71010 00313 78387 52886 58753 32083 81420 61717 76691 47303
59825 34904 28755 46873 11595 62863 88235 37875 93751 95778 18577 80532

The expansion can be computed, but it never ends. Can you memorize the digits of pi up to say the first 10 or 12 places? Rajan did it, through the first 50,000 digits! How could this possibly be done?

We're not sure of the complete answer to that question. We do know, however, that a lot of self-training and self-practice by Rajan was involved. And the training that was done serves in another way to clarify the distinction between fact memory and skill memory. The evidence comes from researchers at Carnegie Mellon University who trained an undergraduate (known as SF), a person with a fairly ordinary memory to begin with, to expand his short-term memory for digits tenfold. We all have a fairly constant-size short-term memory of seven (plus or minus two) items. That is, we can remember up to seven digits almost perfectly but start to forget when the list gets longer. It was the same for SF initially, but SF practiced 1 hour a day, 3 to 5 days a week, for 20 months (more than 230 hours total) trying to remember increasingly more than seven digits. And, guess what? It worked! As practice time went on, SF got to a point where he could recite back about 80 digits read to him by the researchers. So, he learned apparently to expand his short-term memory and to become a kind of mnemonist. Eighty digits might not seem to rival Rajan's 50,000 digits. But remember, Rajan practiced the same digit sequence over and over, whereas SF's 80-digit tests were new to him each time. This example might be dismissed as just a parlor trick if it were not for the fact that close examination of SF revealed how he did it and pointed the way for others to expand their memories.

SF was a serious amateur track athlete. He knew a lot about running times and other track events involving numbers. To expand his digit span, he made strategic use of his existing knowledge of track timing, attempting to relate each set of three to four sequential digits given to him during a practice trial to a known track event such as the average time to run a mile or the world record 50-yard dash. Relating the new (unfamiliar) events to old (familiar) events gave him the leverage he needed to recover long strings of seemingly unrelated digits, resulting in truly impressive memory performance.

Please note: The important thing about SF's performance is not that he added to his repertoire of facts. The important thing is that he acquired a way of using known facts (track times) to retrieve, if only for the moment, a collection of seemingly unrelated digits. Using these known facts requires extra effort and is likely to hinder efficiency. But there is a large retention payoff. SF achieved this feat by practicing retrieval of numbers from his short-term memory and by basing the retrieval process on facts already known. In general, we call this process *retrieval practice*. Retrieval practice results in the acquisition of a memory skill, retrieval skill. It is important to note that skill is quite specific to the type of material trained on (often, but not always, digits). And that observation helps to clarify the difference between fact memory and skill memory. Facts are generally useful and can be applied in a variety of contexts. Skills, in contrast, although generally useful over items within a domain, tend to be specific to those items and not necessarily useful in a different fact domain. Rajan and SF could remember long digit sequences but were close to average on anything else. We will have much more to say about retrieval skill and retrieval practice later.

Use Knowledge You Already Have

What SF accomplished is important in still another way. It suggests another training technique that slows acquisition but boosts memory. Let's see how this technique works in a different context.

Learning almost any new fact can be enhanced by using things you already know, without adding much time to the training process but to the great benefit of memory. SF already knew a lot about track times and found a way to relate new digit sequences to that knowledge. Similarly, you can learn facts about unknown people by associating each unknown person with someone else who is familiar, such as a friend or a relative. Here's how it works. When you need to learn a new set of facts, especially a large set, it is often useful to relate those facts to your preexisting knowledge, if possible.

Suppose you want to learn about opera, specifically facts about composers and the works they created. Attaining this knowledge requires simple, rote learning and is only one component of what you need to know about opera. Full appreciation of opera will, of course, require you to study other, possibly more complicated aspects. You might know very little about composers to begin with, but you should be able to speed up learning this new knowledge by relating composers to people you do know. Suppose you have 12 new composers and operas to commit to memory. Start by thinking of 12 people you are well acquainted with—friends or relatives will do. Then look for helpful connections with the 12 composers and each member of your familiar group. Perhaps your brother Ross reminds you of the composer Rossini (*Barber of Seville*), or your boyfriend, Verne, is easily associated with Verdi (*La Boheme*). Then think of all that you know about Ross or Verne that might help you connect in the opera names, as illustrated in Figure 3.2. "Ah, Ross, he's always combing his hair. Ross and Rossini relate through the Barber of Seville."

You can do the same thing in other ways. Suppose you happen to know a lot about baseball. You can use that knowledge to organize and thus quickly learn a large set of facts about the new task you are trying to master. You start by associating each unfamiliar opera composer, like Wagner, with a well-known baseball player, like Honus Wagner. What you know about baseball will enrich your image of the associated composer. Then the new facts associated with the composer will be mediated by strong preexisting knowledge of the baseball player. Although there is an additional step here, and additional associations might seem to complicate the training task at hand, connections to existing knowledge constitute a desirable difficulty that will actually enhance performance on the new set of facts in terms of both accuracy and speed of responding, especially on a test of retention. Try this technique yourself in another domain using Exercise 3.2.

Use Keywords

One common way to use prior knowledge to learn foreign vocabulary is the *keyword* method. To translate a foreign word into its English equivalent, you first have to think of a word, a keyword, that sounds like or is spelled like the foreign word. Then you form a mental image linking the keyword and the English translation. Two simple steps—associating the foreign word with the keyword and associating the keyword with the English translation—are used in

FIGURE 3.2. Forming New Associations

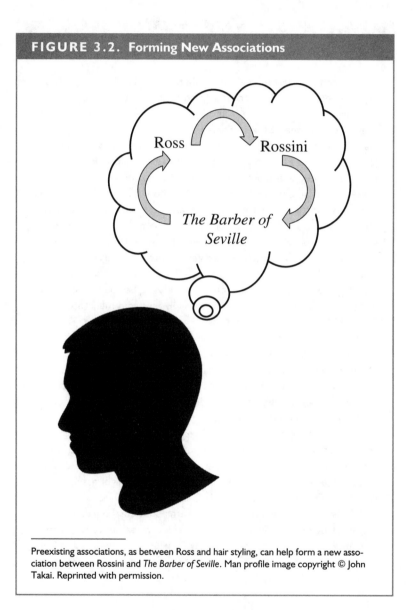

Preexisting associations, as between Ross and hair styling, can help form a new association between Rossini and *The Barber of Seville*. Man profile image copyright © John Takai. Reprinted with permission.

EXERCISE 3.2. Can You Use Your Knowledge of Swimmers to Learn About Classmates?

Often when you start a new class—whether it's in college, high school, or adult education—the teacher asks students to introduce themselves by giving their names and a brief biographical statement. Imagine that in such a class, one of the students has a 2-year-old son and a job as a waiter, another student is a former basketball player who is from New Jersey, and a third student just took a trip to Africa and is in a marching band. Now your class meets for the second time. You wanted to ask the student who had been to Africa a question about that trip, but you can't remember which student took the trip there. You recognize the students, but you can't recall all the biographical information about them. How can you avoid this problem in the future? Are there any tricks you can use to remember who's who and who said what? Here's an exercise that might help you.

Think of some individuals you know well. Maybe you are into swimming, and the individuals you think of are Olympic gold-medal athletes—Michael Phelps, Ryan Lochte, Missy Franklin, Dana Vollmer. The next time you have to learn some facts about a new group of people, who tell their stories in turn, associate each of those people with one of the Olympic swimmers. To see how helpful this technique is, consider dividing the new group of people in half. For half of them (those on the left side of the room), associate each person with a swimmer, and for the other half (those on the right side of the room), don't think of anyone else when listening to their stories. As each person tells his or her story, try to associate the facts with the individual as best you can. For those on the left, also try to associate the person with one of the Olympic swimmers. If the person is a tall, vivacious woman, you might associate her with Missy Franklin. The story of the person probably has nothing to do with Missy Franklin, and the facts you learn about the woman are probably not true of Missy Franklin. Nevertheless, instead of causing confusion, making the association with Missy Franklin might help you to learn the facts about the woman. The next time you get back to the group

---

EXERCISE 3.2. **Can You Use Your Knowledge of Swimmers to Learn About Classmates? (Continued)**

of people, see if you can remember the stories of each one. Did you remember the stories better for the people who had been on the left side of the room previously (who were associated with the swimmers) or for those on the right side of the room (who were not associated with any other people)? Most likely, the associations you made with swimmers helped you learn and remember the facts, so you should do better remembering the stories for the people on the left side of the room than for those on the right side of the room. Try it! You might be surprised at how well you do.

---

this method to replace the one hard step of translating the foreign word into English.

For example, if you want to learn that the French word *bijou* means *jewel,* first find a keyword that sounds or is spelled like *bijou.* How about using *bee* as the keyword, because *bijou* and *bee* have the same initial pronunciation? Then form a mental image that links *bee* to *jewel.* How about an image of a bee sitting on top of a diamond jewel? When given the French word *bijou* (with the first syllable pronounced like bee), it should then be easy for you to translate it to *jewel,* first by thinking of the keyword *bee* and then by retrieving the image of a bee sitting on top of a diamond jewel.

As another example, the French word *pomme* has the English translation *apple.* When given *pomme,* you think of the similar sounding English word *palm,* and then you form an image of an apple being held in the palm of a hand, as in Figure 3.3. Now, whenever you see the French word *pomme,* it should be simple to remember that it means *apple.* Just think of *palm* and then recall your image of the apple being held in the palm of a hand. Exercise 3.3 will give

FIGURE 3.3. Keyword Method for Remembering *Pomme*

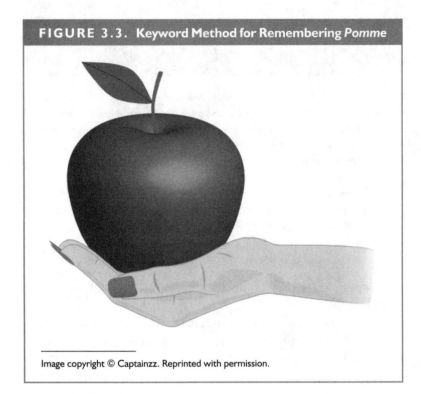

Image copyright © Captainzz. Reprinted with permission.

you some personal experience with using the keyword method and should demonstrate its benefits for memory.

Some words evoke mental pictures more easily than other words—that is, they are more "imageable." How important is the imagability of the keyword? Probably very important. Research has shown that the more easily you can picture a word in your mind, the more easily you can link it to other ideas. Thus, because *bee* is easy to picture in your mind, it helps you link *bijou* and *jewel*. Words that are abstract or difficult to mentally picture, such as *society* or *liberty*, are much less useful as keywords. In fact, in almost any

---

EXERCISE 3.3. The Keyword Method

Let's try using keywords to learn some new foreign vocabulary terms. Remember that in the keyword method, you create a mental image linking the foreign word to its English equivalent.

Imagine that you are trying to learn Spanish without any prior knowledge of the language. See if you can make up your own keywords for the following Spanish–English word pairs: *libro–book, mesa–table, bailar–dance, deporte–sport, carretera–road, suelo–floor.* Can you come up with keywords that might make it easier to learn these new Spanish vocabulary items? For *libro–book,* how about the keyword *library?* Make up two roughly equivalent lists of Spanish–English pairs (use another language if you are already fluent in Spanish). Then see how long it takes to learn one list using the keyword method versus how long it takes to learn the other list without the keyword method. Was there a difference? Did it favor the keyword list? In a majority of cases, it should.

Now wait a week and test yourself again on the vocabulary pairs you learned. Was your test performance better on the list of words learned with the keyword method or on the other list? If the keyword method list led to better test performance, then you showed that it is an effective way to improve retention as well as acquisition.

---

verbal learning task, the more imagable the words to be learned are, the more easily you can learn them.

Why is this? First, pictures are easier to remember than words. If you were presented a list of 20 words and asked to remember them, you would likely remember fewer of them on a later recognition test than if you had been presented a list of 20 pictures corresponding to the 20 words. Something about pictures makes them more memorable or recognizable than words. Remember the old adage, "a picture is worth a 1,000 words."

Second, imageable words are more effective keywords because they are concrete instead of abstract. Concrete words denote concrete objects, like *bee*. In contrast, abstract words like *society* are difficult to image. These words denote something abstract or general and not a single object. It should come as no surprise to discover that concrete words are easier to learn and to remember than abstract words. So, if you can make new material to be learned somehow more concrete (and thus more imageable), you might be able to ease the training burden. That is what the keyword method tries to accomplish, and that is why the keyword method is often quite successful in facilitating the fact-training process.

CONDITIONS THAT *DON'T* SLOW DOWN YOUR LEARNING

There are some ways of training that don't slow you down when learning but still help you retain the learned material. Consider the following strategies.

Group Items Together

One way to improve your memory for a long list of items without slowing you down is to break down the list into a sequence of smaller sublists. Let's say you need to learn a list of 15 digits (maybe a code number for a transaction). The list might seem too difficult to learn as a whole, but if you divide the list into three smaller five-digit groups, or chunks, it will be a lot easier for you to master, especially if you can relate one or more of the chunks to your prior knowledge. In fact, the trained memory expert SF, as noted earlier, was able to learn lists of about 80 random digits, presented successively one digit per second, by breaking down the list into shorter familiar units like running times and dates. If you don't know a lot of running times, you could use familiar birthdays, ages, phone numbers, and addresses instead. This strategy, called *chunking*, might turn you into a memory expert like SF!

Chunking works for almost any material. Instead of digits, consider a string of letters of the alphabet. The average person's short-term memory for letters is just as limited as it is for numerical digits, about seven plus or minus two. In fact, the number 7 shows up commonly as a limitation on all short-term memory. Consider the following string of letters, well beyond our normal letter span. Read the string at a "military" cadence to a friend, one letter at a time about one per second. Then ask your friend to repeat the string:

L-L-A-C-E-R-O-T-Y-S-A-E-E-R-A-S-E-C-N-E-T-N-E-S-T-R-O-H-S

Can your friend repeat the string? Or did your friend think that this was just a bad joke? No one except possibly a mnemonist can repeat back a string of 29 random letters. But now ask the same friend to repeat the following letter string, which consists of the same 29 letters, but in a different order. Once again read the letters with military cadence:

S-H-O-R-T-S-E-N-T-E-N-C-E-S-A-R-E-E-A-S-Y-T-O-R-E-C-A-L-L

If your friend recognizes the chunks in this sequence—words within an easy-to-remember sentence—he or she will have little or no difficulty repeating them. The letters are chunkable into familiar units (words), and the words themselves can be chunked into phrases to form a sentence. In this example, your friend can use chunking and knowledge of the language strategically to perform what would otherwise be a prodigious memory feat. By the way, the word chunks are easier to recognize when the letters are presented visually (as shown previously) than when they are read one at a time—even easier, of course, if you pause or put a space between the words.

Chunks come in different sizes. Three to five items seem like the most useful size. And, of course, not all chunks in the same long list have to be of the same size in order to assist memory. You want the chunk to be meaningful regardless of its size. Exercise 3.4 provides some insight into how to determine the size just right for a chunk.

Use the Same Procedures in Training and in Subsequent Tests

To maximize your retention of what you learn, be sure to test yourself under the same conditions as in training. If you trained in a particular place, test in the same place for maximal retention. If you trained with a particular order of materials, test in that same order. The converse also works and is often more practical, because we usually have less control over the testing situation than we have over the training situation. So, if you know how you will be tested in the future, then design your training to match the circumstances of testing as closely as possible. What is crucial in terms of matching training and testing conditions is that the procedural information (the skill) be the same. It is not crucial to match the declarative information (the facts). See Exercise 3.5 on differences in memory for procedural and declarative information.

This approach works beautifully for immediate tests of retention. Interestingly, however, if you want to promote longer term retention, retesting under varied conditions might work to your advantage. More will be said about this possibility when we discuss the generalizability of training. How you should test for retention depends on what you are trying to accomplish.

Test Yourself Instead of Restudying

Tests are usually thought of as assessment tools rather than training tools. But there is increasing evidence that people often learn as

EXERCISE 3.4. Chunking—How Big Should the Chunks Be?

When you are confronted with a daunting memory task and you want to use chunking, how big should your chunks be? Let's say you want to break down a long list of words into smaller sublists or chunks, just as the memory expert SF did with lists of digit strings. How long should those sublists be? The sublists don't all have to be the same length, and it should be helpful to find out what the optimal chunk size is for you. Here's an exercise that should help you make some decisions about how to use chunking.

Try to learn three different lists of 24 randomly selected words in three different ways. For the first list, break it down into four chunks of six words each. For the second list, break it down into six chunks of four words each. And for the third list, break it down into eight chunks of three words each. For each chunk in each list, try to form a sentence containing all of the words in that chunk. Study the lists one at a time. After a certain length of study time, say 10 minutes, record how many of the words you recalled correctly from each list. Did you recall more words when you used six-word chunks, four-word chunks, or three-word chunks? After some practice at chunking, many people find that longer chunks (but not too long) work best. Note also that the best chunk size for words formed into sentences might not be the best chunk size for other material. So you might want to try this exercise again for other material, like numerical digit strings, that you need to remember to see what the best chunk size is in that case. Of course, something other than sentences will be required to organize digits. SF used track times that he had great familiarity with.

People are better at retaining procedural information (that is, skills) than declarative information (that is, facts). To demonstrate this, get a copy of your state's automobile *Drivers' Manual,* the book that drivers use to study for their written drivers' test. Read the manual, and then answer the following questions. The procedural questions have to do with actual driving operations (skills), and the declarative questions address supplementary material (facts).[1]

Question 1a (declarative): If you are moving into the state, you must obtain your new license plates within ___ days after becoming a resident.

Question 1b (procedural): The state speed limit in any residence district is ___ mph.

Question 2a (declarative): Driving under the influence (DUI) is presumed by blood alcohol content of ___ parts in 10,000.

Question 2b (procedural): Under normal conditions a good rule of thumb is to follow no closer than one car length for every ___ mph of speed.

Question 3a (declarative): License plates must be fastened horizontally in a manner to prevent swinging at a height of at least ___ inches from the ground.

Question 3b (procedural): When parking is permitted, your vehicle must be within ___ inches of the curb.

The declarative and procedural questions in each pair have the same answers in many states, although they might be different in yours. Here are the common answers:

Question 1: 30
Question 2: 10
Question 3: 12

Did you do better on the declarative questions or the procedural questions? Typically, experienced drivers answer correctly more procedural questions than declarative questions. Experience with the motoric, perceptual, and cognitive procedures required when driving promotes long-term retention of the answers to the procedural questions.

---

[1]These examples are derived from an experiment by Jensen, M. B., & Healy, A. F. (1998). Retention of procedural and declarative information from the *Colorado Drivers' Manual.* In M. J. Intons-Peterson & D. Best (Eds.), *Memory distortions and their prevention* (pp. 113–124). Mahwah, NJ: Erlbaum.

much from taking tests as they learn from pure study—and sometimes even more. This phenomenon has been referred to as the *testing effect*. In skill learning tasks, such as playing a particular passage on the piano, study and test are usually integrated into the trial-by-trial acquisition procedure, with each trial necessarily including a testing component. Thus, the testing effect is mostly limited to fact-learning tasks, although mental practice of a skill (or even observation of someone else carrying out the skill) might be considered a form of studying without testing.

The testing effect is powerful because it requires people to retrieve information from memory. Memory retrieval itself is a skill. The more you do it, the better you'll become at it, at least within the context of the practice task. Just as it can be difficult to find a book in the library, it can be difficult to find information stored in your mind. Practicing the memory retrieval process will enable you to do it more quickly and accurately in the future.

Certain types of tests require a more elaborate retrieval skill than do others. Short-answer essay or fill-in-the-blank questions put a heavier burden on memory than do true/false or multiple-choice questions. The latter question types don't require that you find the answer in your memory because the answer is always embedded in the test itself. But for fill-in-the-blank questions, you have to generate the correct response or find it in your mind. Questions like these provide a more helpful form of retrieval practice, which you wouldn't get from other types of tests. So, when you want to increase your retrieval skill, we recommend that you test yourself (or have your study partner or coach test you) with fill-in-the-blank or short-answer essay questions.

Testing is not the only way to provide for retrieval practice. Now that you know how important retrieval practice is, you can do it when you are trying to learn something new. Let's say, for example, that you are asked to give a talk someplace, perhaps your church or school. You might write out the talk completely because you want to be sure that you know exactly what you want to say and that your talk will fit into the time slot provided. How should you learn the talk so that you can say it fluently without consulting any notes? You could read it over and over, multiple times. But such a strategy would not provide for retrieval practice. It would not force you to find in your mind the ideas that you want to bring up in the talk. Instead, put your notes aside and try to give the talk without them. You might miss some of the points or not say them in the optimal manner. But try to do the best you can without looking at your notes. Now read the notes to check and see what you left out. Keep doing this procedure, retrieving without notes and then checking the notes, over and over. This type of practice will help you by forcing you to exercise the needed retrieval skill. Speaking without notes is not as easy as just reading your notes, but the added difficulty will be beneficial for later performance.

The same kind of retrieval practice can be used on other occasions as well. For example, if you're training on the piano, you may be scheduled to participate in a recital before an audience. You should use retrieval practice with the piano piece, mentally tapping all of the notes in the piece without looking at the music. That practice might help you learn the particular piece better, so that you can perform it well at the recital. But it might also help you improve your general piano playing skill so that you can perform other pieces better too.

Retrieval practice might be helpful not only for learning the information you are studying at the moment but also for learning other material as well—at least within the same domain. The skill of retrieving things from your memory can be enhanced just like any other skill. In fact, it is one of the most important skills you can develop. Try to improve that skill, and you will see benefits throughout your life! Exercise 3.6 will give you some experience with retrieval practice.

Study Material at Its Most Meaningful Level

New information to be learned can be processed in different ways or at different levels of meaningfulness. "Deep" training tasks, which cause you to think about the meaning of the material, help you remember the material better than "shallow" training tasks, which lead you to consider only superficial aspects of the material. Remember Spinoza's doctrine: The more meaningful something is, the better it will be retained.

Consider a situation in which you need to learn a list of words, perhaps the names of all of the swim teams in your district. What can you do to make that memory task easy? Divide the list in half. Process the first half of the names deeply. For example, when learning those names, think about whether each one of them is an animal. If the name is *shark*, you would decide "yes," but if it is *wave*, you would decide "no." Now go through the second half of the names in a shallow manner. For example, when learning each of those names, see if it has five or more letters. In this case, again, you would decide "yes" for *shark* and "no" for *wave*, but on a more shallow basis. Now try to recall the complete list of swim teams. How many names did you remember from the first half, and how many from the second half? Most likely, you could remember more of the team names from the first half of the list, which you processed deeply, than from the second half of the list, which you processed in a more shallow manner. The moral of this story is that you should think deeply, considering the meaning, about any material that you are trying to learn. That deep processing will allow you to learn the material better so that you can remember it in the future.

EXERCISE 3.6. Practice Retrieving From Memory

Memory retrieval is a major skill in the execution of all fact-learning tasks. Practicing the skill will serve you well in all your training activities. So, let's do some exercises where you use the skill of retrieving from memory. First, come up with a list of popular songs like "Moon River" or "Stardust." For each one, try to retrieve the lyrics, word for word, from memory. You can always check yourself by searching for the songs on the Internet. Now for each one, try to retrieve the melody from memory. If you can play the piano, try it there. If you can play the clarinet or guitar, play the tune on that instrument. If you're musically illiterate, like many of us, just humming the tune will be fine for purposes of this exercise. Again, if you want to check yourself, the Internet has many songs with their tunes as well as their lyrics.

Tired of popular songs? Let's try to retrieve another kind of information from memory. Can you repeat verbatim your school "fight" song, usually sung at sporting events, or your school alma mater, or the Pledge of Allegiance? How did you do? Did you find all of the words in your memory? What about telephone numbers? Can you remember your first telephone number? What about the telephone numbers of your friends and relatives? Try to find them in memory. Here's something else to search for: the street names in your neighborhood. How good are you at remembering them? Can you remember the street names in a place you lived a while ago? That should be more challenging, but that information should be stored someplace in your memory.

Practice finding information in your mind, and checking to be sure you got it right, helps you improve the skill of memory retrieval, although the effect might be limited to the type of material you practice on. The next time you have to find something buried in your memory, you might be able to do so more accurately and rapidly if you take retrieval practice seriously.

Generate Information Rather Than Just Read It

One important way to process information at a deep level, and thus to facilitate its retention, is to try generating the information yourself, rather than just reading or copying it. Let's say you want to remember which composer created which opera. You will probably learn faster and remember the pairs better if, rather than just reading the pairs (e.g., *La Boheme*–Puccini), you attempt for each opera to generate the composer's name given only the first three letters of that name. For example, *La Boheme*–Puc____. There is something about having to think about the pairings that helps to solidify the answer in your memory. Of course, you should check your answer so that errors can be corrected.

Here's another example. Suppose that you want to remember the numerical answers to a set of simple arithmetic problems. If you merely copy down the problems and the answers, you would be much less likely to remember them than if you copy the problems and then generate the answers yourself by calculating them. So, if you see the problems and answers and then verify the answers, you will remember the answers because to verify them you have to do the mental calculations yourself. On the other hand, if you see only the problems and generate the answers but use a calculator to compute the answers rather than compute them in your head, you won't do well at retaining the answers. Although some people rely on computers to do calculations for them, this is probably not a good strategy if you need to remember the calculations. Using your head to make those calculations increases your ability to remember them later.

Generating information (rather than just reading it) seems to have a positive benefit for memory on all kinds of material. And it works even when the generation task is very easy. Let's say you have to remember a particular word, *bird*. You will remember it better if you have to transpose the first two letters to form the word (e.g., transpose the first two letters of *ibrd* to form the word *bird*) than if you just read the word correctly spelled. Even if you are told ahead of time to transpose the letters (thus making the task rather trivial), that task will help you remember the word. What is most crucial is that the task leads you to engage in a mental consideration of the material to be learned and that this consideration should promote deeper processing and better retention of the material. Although we have used very simple training examples in this description, you might find that generating information is especially valuable when your fact-learning task is difficult and your progress has been slow. Exercise 3.7 shows the memory benefits of generating information.

Test Yourself During Periods of Disuse

One important thing to keep in mind when you are trying to improve your memory for facts is what happens during a retention interval. The *retention interval* is the time between when you are given some information to remember (acquisition) and when you are required to retrieve it (retention). Memory decays for all of us as time passes. It is much harder to retrieve information after a long retention interval than after a short one. You need to know that most of the forgetting occurs rapidly, actually in the first few minutes of the retention interval. So if you can hold onto some information for a few minutes, you will probably be able to remember it for a longer period of time.

One way to help you cope with a long retention interval is to test yourself in the middle of it. That will protect your memory against the decay of time. How far apart should your tests be spaced? The best spacing makes the tests not too easy, but not too hard. That is, you don't want the tests to be spaced so far apart that you can't remember anything during those tests, but you also don't want them to be so close together that you remember everything very easily. Information that is still active in short-term memory

EXERCISE 3.7. Generating Information: Does It Work for You?

Generating information is a powerful tool for making any text material more meaningful and more memorable. To see whether this works for you, let's consider the task of learning capitals of all of the states in the United States. Let's make it a bit easier by giving you the names of the capitals and having you learn the name of the state associated with each capital. You probably already know many of these capital–state associations, but it might be useful for you to know all of them. Figure 3.4 provides the 50 state–capital pairs with the states listed in alphabetical order. Divide the list into halves, with each set including 25 pairs. Study both halves of the list for 15 minutes.

For the first set, copy down each capital–state pair as your way of studying it a second time. For the other set, cover up all of the state names, leaving just the capitals. Now for each capital, write it down and try to generate the state associated with it. You can check yourself after you have made your best guess by looking at the state name. When you finish generating and checking the second set of state names, take a test on all of the state names. Again cover up the state names, this time for all 50 states. For each capital, write down the state associated with it. How did you do on this test? Did you do better on the second set of 25 pairs, where you had to generate the state during training, than you did on the first set, where you only read the state during training? Did generating information help you remember the pairs?

As a further test of the effectiveness of generating information, list all 50 states in alphabetical order, as in Figure 3.4. Instead of recalling the state for each capital, you should recall the capital for each state, which should be a harder task because it requires you to use backward (state— capital) associations. See how many states you can write down the capital for. Did you do better this time with the 25 states that had been in the generating-information task or with those that had been in the read-only task during training? If generating information helps you on both the easier task (giving state names to capitals) and the more difficult task (giving capitals to state names), you will have demonstrated to yourself how powerful generating information can be as a tool to improve memory. Believe us, it will come in handy in a lot of fact-training tasks.

FIGURE 3.4. States and Capitals

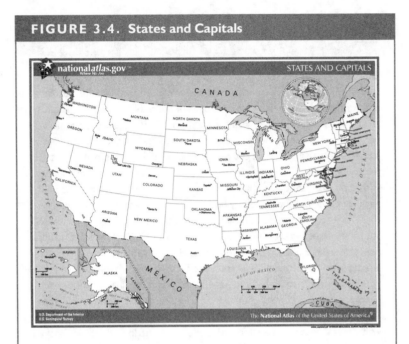

Alabama	Montgomery	Delaware	Dover
Alaska	Juneau	Florida	Tallahassee
Arizona	Phoenix	Georgia	Atlanta
Arkansas	Little Rock	Hawaii	Honolulu
California	Sacramento	Idaho	Boise
Colorado	Denver	Illinois	Springfield
Connecticut	Hartford	Indiana	Indianapolis

Map reprinted from nationalatlas.gov. In the public domain.

FIGURE 3.4. States and Capitals (Continued)

Iowa	Des Moines	North Carolina	Raleigh
Kansas	Topeka	North Dakota	Bismarck
Kentucky	Frankfort	Ohio	Columbus
Louisiana	Baton Rouge	Oklahoma	Oklahoma City
Maine	Augusta	Oregon	Salem
Maryland	Annapolis	Pennsylvania	Harrisburg
Massachusetts	Boston	Rhode Island	Providence
Michigan	Lansing	South Carolina	Columbia
Minnesota	St. Paul	South Dakota	Pierre
Mississippi	Jackson	Tennessee	Nashville
Missouri	Jefferson City	Texas	Austin
Montana	Helena	Utah	Salt Lake City
Nebraska	Lincoln	Vermont	Montpelier
Nevada	Carson City	Virginia	Richmond
New Hampshire	Concord	Washington	Olympia
New Jersey	Trenton	West Virginia	Charleston
New Mexico	Santa Fe	Wisconsin	Madison
New York	Albany	Wyoming	Cheyenne

requires little or no effort to remember. The benefits of testing come primarily from having to work to remember.

But time alone, and the decay of memory over time, are not the only sources of memory loss. Another even more powerful source of memory loss is called *interference*. Interference is caused by events that are similar to, or confusable with, the information you're trying to remember. For example, maybe you need to remember a new 10-digit phone number. You would like to remember that number from the time you hear it spoken by operator assistance to the time you get your cell phone ready to dial it. If only 30 seconds have passed between receiving and dialing the number, you should have no problem. But how about if during that 30-second period a friend asks you an unrelated question or, even worse, gives you another 10-digit phone number? In either case, there is likely to be some confusion. And confusion produces interference.

Sometimes confusion arises from prior events rather than from present events. In either case, try to avoid it. One thing you can do is space out the learning of similar material as much as possible. The easiest way to avoid the interference from learning a lot of similar lists is to take short breaks between trying to memorize the lists.

Combine Two Tasks Into One

Earlier, when we discussed part training, we noted that some skills that people learn are really combinations of simple skills done simultaneously. Think, for example, of learning to play a new piece on the piano. Your two hands are doing quite different things. You can, in fact, practice the right-hand parts and the left-hand parts separately, and then later put them together. In music, the two parts are quite compatible, and it usually isn't too difficult to integrate them. The integrated whole task is often referred to as the *functional task,* in the sense that it functions as a whole activity on its own, not as two separate activities.

But some tasks are not easily integrated. We often find our-
selves occupied by two competing tasks at the same time. For example, many people listen to music while they are reading or trying
to reconcile their checkbook. Students often watch TV at the same
time as they are doing their homework or studying for an exam.
And when people are driving, they often hold a conversation with
someone who is in the car with them. In fact, although we certainly
don't recommend it, when some people are driving they carry on a
cell phone conversation with someone else. Alternatively, as shown
in Figure 3.5, they might even send and receive text messages while
they are driving! Distracted driving can lead to serious accidents. In

FIGURE 3.5. There are Limits to Multitasking

Texting while driving is not a great idea. No one, absolutely no one, can multitask
these two complex skills. There ought to be a law against it in every state. Image
copyright © Kyle Strayer. Reprinted with permission.

fact, driving and talking on the cell phone is similar in terms of the degree of impairment to driving while intoxicated. So don't do it!

Despite this warning, we acknowledge that there are many times when doing two things at once is necessary. This is called *multitasking,* and some people claim they are quite good at it, as we discuss in detail in Chapter 5. Take those claims with a grain of salt. But you can, with practice, get better at multitasking. If you diligently practice doing the same two things at the same time over an extended period, you will definitely improve. In most cases, though, you will never perform as well as you will on either of the separate tasks alone.

Suppose, in your training, you develop some skill in doing two tasks simultaneously. Both tasks are based on their own set of procedures, which are unlikely to be the same or overlapping. Performance on a test depends heavily on which set of procedures is required by the test. If you want to optimize your performance on a test, be sure that the test requires the same procedures as engaged during training. Or alternatively, in preparing for a test in multitasking, be sure that practice during training contains the same procedures as will be used in the test. How these processes work together to shape your performance is illustrated in Exercise 3.8.

Don't Train More Than Necessary

When should you stop training and move onto something else? You might think that the time to stop training is after the task is mastered, perhaps because you've reached a specific performance criterion. However, even when you reach a point of errorless performance, there is more to be gained from further practice. For example, the amount of effort you need to expend might decline with further practice, even if speed and accuracy have already been maximized. In tennis, the less effort that is required of your own strokes, the more effort you can devote to following your opponent's moves. So "over-

EXERCISE 3.8. Combining Two Tasks Into One

We are going to investigate the possibilities of multitasking by trying, through training, to turn two different tasks into a single functional task.

Take two tasks, like practicing scales on a piano and making time estimation judgments. Can you do them both at the same time? Start by checking your watch and writing down on a piece of paper the exact time. Then, without looking at your watch again (or any other clock), decide when exactly 2 minutes have elapsed. While you are waiting for the time to pass, you should perform scales on the piano. When you think 2 minutes have passed, check your watch to see how close to 2 minutes you were. Did you underestimate or overestimate the time? By how much? If you try this same combination of tasks repeatedly, you'll become increasingly more accurate at estimating a 2-minute interval. You've acquired by training an ability to do time estimation quite well even while engaged simultaneously in a secondary task. You've done some successful multitasking. Incidentally, practicing scales is not the only secondary task you might use. If you don't have a piano handy or you don't have any idea how to play scales on a piano, try a different task. A simple one that almost any adult can do these days is typing on a keyboard. Type the letters of the alphabet, in order, starting at some arbitrary point. Your performance on your time estimation test should more or less be the same as if you did another secondary task (like playing scales on a piano).

Here's an interesting follow-up test: Try the primary task of time estimation alone with no secondary task. In other words, try to estimate when 2 minutes have elapsed without practicing piano scales at the same time. How well did you do on this test? You might expect to do better on time estimation because you can fully concentrate on that task and don't have to worry about doing anything else. But in fact, it's likely that you will do worse than when you were doing both tasks. Why did your time estimation performance suffer when a difficult secondary task was removed? The answer is that the procedures you learned during training involved not only the time estimation task, but also the requirements of the piano scales task. We described the two tasks as primary and secondary. However, in fact, what you really learned was to combine two different tasks into one functional task. In the combined task, it is likely

(continued)

EXERCISE 3.8. Combining Two Tasks Into One
(*Continued*)

that you were able to judge that 2 minutes had passed by considering how many times you went through the scales or what note you stopped on to make your time estimate. But when you were given the seemingly easier task of estimating time alone, without playing scales on the piano, you did not have those same landmarks to use as reference points. You had to use somewhat different procedures to estimate time, and this difference necessarily set your time estimation skill back a notch.

The forgoing exercise demonstrates that when you want to train on any new task, be sure to consider what you'll be required to do in the background during your test of performance on that task. Try to train with the same tasks that you anticipate doing at the test. Please note that although this is a form of multitasking, some tasks don't combine well. Don't try to learn how to send text messages while operating dangerous machinery or driving a car. You'll be courting disaster. Besides, at least in some progressive states, it's against the law to text and drive at the same time (although this law is rarely enforced).

---

learning" (practicing beyond that necessary to reach a set criterion level of performance) can be beneficial.

But we do not recommend overlearning, at least not immediately after you've reached your criterion level. Overlearning generates diminishing return benefits. You gain a lot at the beginning of practice, but then you gain less and less as you practice more and more. Overlearning might produce some improvement, but it will be minimal. So is overlearning worth the effort? It depends on your training goal. If you want to perform like an expert, overlearning might be worthwhile, especially in skill-based tasks. But for most tasks, especially those involving fact learning, overlearning is not advisable. Moreover, if you expect to perform tests after training, the tests will serve the same purpose as overlearning.

THE TAKEAWAY

Durability of trained material is the second leg of our training stool. What we learn is of no value if it is quickly forgotten. This chapter outlines things you can do during training and testing to enhance durability and to ensure that you remember the material later. Table 3.1 summarizes these training principles. The next

TABLE 3.1. Training Principles for Durability: How to Retain What You Learn	
Purpose: Retaining acquisition effects over a period of nonpractice	
Principle	**Application**
Conditions that slow down your learning	
Task difficulty	Add complications to the training task.
Mnemonists	Follow the procedures used by memory experts.
Strategic use of knowledge	Use knowledge you already have.
Memory strategies	Use keywords.
Conditions that don't slow down your learning	
Chunking	Group items together.
Procedural reinstatement	Use the same procedures in training and in subsequent tests.
Testing	Test yourself instead of restudying.
Depth of processing	Study material at its most meaningful level.
Generation	Generate information rather than just read it.
Periodic restudy	Test yourself during periods of disuse.
Functional task	Combine two tasks into one.
Overlearning	Don't train more than necessary.

chapter addresses the third leg of the stool, training generalizability. In a way, as you will see, it is the most difficult stool leg to deal with. It is also the leg about which training science has given us the least amount of help. Still, there are some things that work to promote training generalizability, and these things provide a basis for transferring what you've learned to new and different situations.

CHAPTER 4

HOW TO APPLY WHAT YOU LEARN TO NEW SITUATIONS: INCREASING THE GENERALIZABILITY OF TRAINING

> *An expert is one who comes to know more and more about less and less, until he or she knows all there is to know about absolutely nothing.*
>
> —Common Witticism

Don't take the above epigram too seriously. It's meant to be funny but also to suggest that expert performance requires not just a lot of training and a good memory for what has been trained, but also the ability to generalize to novel situations, beyond the training situation.

WHAT IS AN EXPERT ANYWAY?

Ever watch the television show *Antiques Roadshow*, pictured in Figure 4.1, a program carried by the PBS channel on which antiques brought in by locals are evaluated by expert appraisers? If so, have you been impressed by the detailed descriptions or analyses given by appraisers of esoteric items such as pieces of Native American jewelry, firearms from the Civil War era, and paintings by artists you've never heard of? How is it that these appraisers know so much (approximately 50,000 chunks of information according to Nobel

FIGURE 4.1. Application of Expert Knowledge

Antiques Roadshow appraiser Stephen Fletcher startles the owner of a Simon Willard clock (circa 1823) by estimating its value. Photo courtesy of ANTIQUES ROADSHOW/ WGBH-TV Boston, © 1997–2013 WGBH Educational Foundation.

Prize winner Herb Simon) about seemingly obscure objects and can generalize that knowledge to previously unseen items, to the surprise and delight or amazement of their owners? The appraisers are truly experts in their field. How did they get that way?

Well, by now, you surely know at least part of the answer. To become an expert in any field takes a lot of training. As we noted in Chapter 1, experts like these appraisers have had a lot of experience and practice, maybe as many as 10,000 hours' worth. They have acquired more knowledge and skill in that field than most of us thought existed. Further, as a part of the job, they have found it necessary on a regular basis to use what they know. The

Antiques Roadshow appraisers have learned and must remember what is necessary to evaluate antiques.

But there is a bit more to it. Learning and remembering alone are not enough. Expert appraisers can, in most cases, evaluate accurately an object that might be on the fringes of their expertise, objects they have never seen before. They must be able to apply training to completely novel items or situations. In other words, the appraisers' knowledge and skill must be generalizable, or transferable, so as to be used successfully throughout a given field. A true expert must not only acquire and remember the facts and procedures of the field, but also be able to transfer all that knowledge to almost any situation within the field. We rarely, if ever, encounter the same situation more than once. As the ancient Greek philosopher Heraclitus noted many years ago, "No man ever steps in the same river twice." In this chapter, we move to the third leg of the training stool, *generalizability*. We discuss how to make training generalizable so that we can transfer what we've learned to new circumstances, contrary to what the epigram might imply.

One reason why generalizability is so important is that *durability* (the ability to remember what you learn) is not always coupled with generalizability. In fact, the skills we remember the best are often the most difficult to transfer to other situations. If we change only a small requirement of the skill, we sometimes find that we have to start our training over again because we cannot apply anything that we've learned previously to these new requirements. In other words, durable skills are typically highly specific to the conditions under which training occurred. Thus, we need to consider how we can overcome this high degree of specificity. What can we do during training to ensure or to promote skill generality?

This is a very difficult problem because there are only a few known methods to help you learn transferable skills. Unfortunately, there are not many things we can do to increase the generalizability of skill training. Nevertheless, there are some possibilities, and we consider them here.

Although trained skills lack generalizability, trained knowledge (that is, facts) is usually highly generalizable. An expert appraiser is often able to use facts learned about a similar object to evaluate another object that he or she has never seen before. Because facts are already highly generalizable, we concentrate our efforts in this chapter on ways to improve the generalizability of skill training.

How do you assess the generalizability of a newly trained skill? As described earlier, you do it in what we've called a *transfer session*. In the transfer session, you have to perform a new task, different from the one you trained on but similar to it in certain ways. The difference between the training and the transfer tasks could be in the task itself or in the task environment. If the environment stays the same, then the conditions that prompt the task might change. Or these conditions might stay the same, but the way you respond might differ. Finally, only the setting might change.

To evaluate performance in the transfer task, we look at both how accurately and how quickly the new task is performed. We also examine how long it takes to reach a certain level of performance on the new task. The question is, does training on the original task affect in any way, hopefully positively, training on the new task? When the two tasks are similar, we expect that training on the old task will help training on the new task (positive transfer), but we need to test to be sure. Some changes between acquisition and transfer tasks might actually produce a harmful result (negative transfer). Obviously it's important to know when transfer has the positive effect we would like to promote and when it does not. Exercise 4.1 is meant to demonstrate both positive and negative transfer. The principles we discuss next will help you improve generalizability.

EXERCISE 4.1. Positive and Negative Transfer

When learning one task facilitates learning or performance on a second task, we say that there is "positive transfer." In contrast, when learning one task impedes learning or performance on a second task, we say there is "negative transfer." Both types of transfer effects occur with some frequency in everyday life. Let's do an exercise to determine whether positive or negative transfer occurs when two similar tasks are used in an acquisition session followed by a transfer session.

Do you know how to type on a standard computer keyboard? Do you think you could improve your typing speed with practice? Try this. Type the following passage (part of Lincoln's Gettysburg address), five times capitalizing every other letter. (Again, remember to disable the auto-correct feature on your computer before you do any typing exercise.)

> Four score and seven years ago our fathers brought forth on this continent, a new nation, conceived in Liberty, and dedicated to the proposition that all men are created equal. Now we are engaged in a great civil war, testing whether that nation, or any nation so conceived and so dedicated, can long endure. We are met on a great battlefield of that war. We have come to dedicate a portion of that field, as a final resting place for those who here gave their lives that that nation might live. It is altogether fitting and proper that we should do this.

Capitalizing every other letter will slow you down at first, because that's not the way you were originally trained, but your speed and accuracy will pick up. This part of the exercise is the acquisition session because you are acquiring the new skill.

Now for transfer. Type the same passage, but this time capitalize every other word (instead of every other letter). How did you do? Do you think you are better or worse off in the transfer task because of the prior acquisition session practice? To answer this question completely you would really need to compare transfer performance with and without a

(continued)

EXERCISE 4.1. Positive and Negative Transfer
(*Continued*)

prior acquisition session. In other words you would have to know how you would have done on the word capitalization task if you had not had an acquisition session on letter capitalization. Thus, a complete answer to this question is impossible.

However, we can get an approximate answer to this question by examining our performance during the acquisition session. Let's say your transfer performance was far and away better than your acquisition performance. That result would suggest positive transfer from one typing task to another. Positive transfer might be expected because you learned during acquisition how to alternate between capital and regular text. On the other hand, you might find that your transfer performance was a lot worse than your acquisition performance, which would suggest negative transfer from one typing task to another. Negative transfer might be expected because the alternation for words is different from that for letters. Another possibility is no difference between acquisition and transfer performance, suggesting neither positive nor negative transfer. These are all possible outcomes of your exercise, and, no matter what actually happens, you can get a sense from this exercise about the range of possible transfer effects and about the generalizability of the skill you trained up on during acquisition.

HOW TO ENHANCE POSITIVE TRANSFER

Change the Conditions of Practice Periodically

The best method to ensure generalizability is to vary the acquisition practice regimen—that is, make it as broad and comprehensive as possible. Practice can be varied in many ways, but there are two basic categories of variation: variation in terms of the environment and variation in the task itself.

Consider first the environment. Say you are practicing the skill of puzzle solving or, more specifically, anagram puzzle solving (where you rearrange scrambled letters to form a familiar word). You could practice anagrams at home, at work, at the doctor's office, on a bus, or in a plane. The more different places you practice, the more generalizable your skill will be. You will be better at solving anagrams in new locations if you practice solving them in a variety of locations. The skill is the same regardless of the environment.

Another idea is to change the equipment used for a task. In the case of anagrams, the task could be conducted with paper and pencil or with a computer. In other cases, like practicing the piano, there could be even more variation in equipment because there could be many differences from one piano to another. Likewise, for the skill of learning how to drive a car, there could be a lot of variation in the equipment because cars differ in so many ways. If you expect to be required to perform a task using a variety of equipment, then it would be best to practice the skill in advance with as many different types of equipment as are available to you. For example, if you want to be prepared to play on any piano, it would be best to practice in advance on a variety of pianos. And if you want to be prepared to drive a new car (say, if you anticipate renting a car in the future), it would be best to get experience driving a variety of cars. This variability in practice will enable you to perform your skill without a hitch, even when there is a change in equipment.

But variations in the environment might not help to improve your ability to perform another related task. To increase the generalizability from one task to another, you will have to vary the task itself rather than where or how it is performed. For example, the anagram task might vary in terms of the number of letters involved. You could practice just five-letter anagrams, or you could practice three-letter anagrams, five-letter anagrams, and seven-letter anagrams. That variation in practice should help you with a new anagram length, like four letters or six letters. Even lengths outside the range you practiced (like eight letters) should benefit from variation in the practice length. If you expect to be required to solve anagrams of all different lengths, then it would be best for you to vary the length of the anagrams you use in practice. Try Exercise 4.2 to see the relative merits of fixed and varied practice.

EXERCISE 4.2. Fixed Versus Varied Practice—Which Is Better for You?

Have you ever played the game of beanbag toss? One of the strongest pieces of scientific evidence for the advantages of variability of practice comes from an experiment using that game. If you want to see if varied practice is better than fixed practice, you can do a miniexperiment that in effect replicates this classic experiment. Get out a set of four beanbags and a marker. If you don't have any beanbags or markers you probably can make them yourself. Beanbags are just small sealed bags (plastic storage bags will do) containing dried beans or pellets. A marker can take many different forms and is used simply to indicate the goal or target location. The exercise will work best with a group of people, perhaps a group of kids. So if you want to entertain a group at a party where you play some games, this would be a good game to consider.

Divide your participants into two groups or teams—varied and fixed. To the best of your ability, make sure the two groups are equal in terms of gender, age, and hand–eye coordination. Each group will practice throwing beanbags at the marker from a starting line that you should draw. You could use a stick to indicate the starting line if you are playing outside or someplace where you don't want to or can't draw a line on the floor. For the varied group, have the participants practice throwing the four beanbags at a marker 3 feet away from the starting line. Then move the marker so that it is 5 feet away, and have them practice throwing the four beanbags to this marker at the new distance.

EXERCISE 4.2. Fixed Versus Varied Practice—Which Is Better for You? (*Continued*)

For the fixed group, also give the participants the chance to practice throwing the four beanbags two times each, but in this case keep the marker at the same distance of 4 feet throughout practice.

Now practice is over and competition begins. Place the marker 4 feet away from the starting line (intermediate to the two distances used for the varied group and the only distance used for the fixed group). Let all of your participants, those in each group, throw a beanbag at the marker, and use a yard stick to measure the distance each bag lands from the marker. You might want to give each participant two, three, or four tries. See which group gets the best average score in terms of the distance from the marker for all of their tries. The fixed group did all of their practice at the distance used for the competition, whereas the varied group did none of their practice at the competition distance. Which group do you think will do better? Most likely, the varied group will do better than the fixed group, even though the varied group had no prior practice at the competition distance. Is that what you found? If so, you have conducted a convincing demonstration of the effectiveness of variable practice.

What you've done here is collect some data from other people, the participants in your miniexperiment. To convert this procedure to an exercise, you'll need to practice yourself under fixed and varied conditions. You'll have to do some balancing of the conditions of practice. For example, first practice under varied conditions, then test yourself; next practice under fixed conditions and again test. To balance, you will next want to practice under fixed conditions once more followed by a test, and then practice again under varied conditions and test once again. This might not be a perfect experimental design, but if you average your scores under the two fixed trials and the two varied trials separately, you should come away with some idea of whether fixed or varied practice works better for you.

Use a Few Selected Examples to Define a Domain

Knowledge is typically categorizable by domains. There is, for example, musical knowledge or knowledge about American history. Often acquiring a little bit of knowledge helps you acquire more knowledge within the same domain. This is called *seeding the knowledge base*. That is, the first few facts that you learn provide the seeds for expanding what you know, your knowledge base.

Here's a concrete example. Much knowledge and many skills involve numbers and making numerical estimates. Sometimes we have to estimate how much time it will take for us to do a particular task, how many calories are contained in a given food, how much it costs for a given product, or how far away a given location is from our home or workplace. Making these kinds of numerical estimates is a skill that can be learned. It has been shown that one way to improve this skill is through the technique of seeding.

To use seeding, you need to practice estimating quantities in a given domain, checking your accuracy after each time. That type of practice enables you to make more accurate estimates in the future for other quantities in the same domain. For example, in the domain of geography, if you want to learn how to estimate the population of countries, you could train by estimating country populations for a fixed small set of countries, checking the accuracy of each estimate after you make it, as illustrated in Figure 4.2. If seeding works, you should now be better able to estimate populations for countries that you did not encounter during practice. That is, the seeding practice on one set of country facts should be generalizable to facts about another set of countries. Your estimates of population for the new countries should be more accurate following seeding than they would be without the seeding practice.

But don't think that seeding practice with country populations can help you in estimating other quantitative facts about countries,

FIGURE 4.2. Seeding

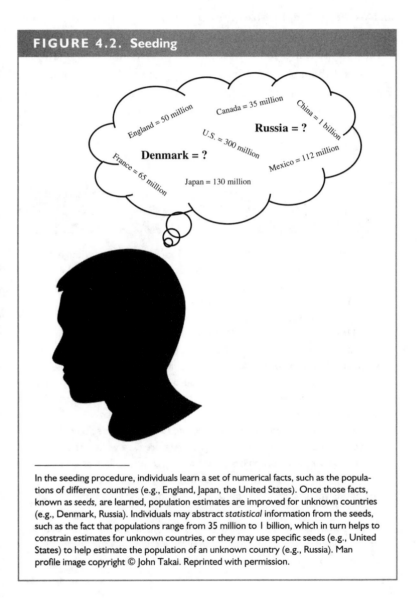

In the seeding procedure, individuals learn a set of numerical facts, such as the populations of different countries (e.g., England, Japan, the United States). Once those facts, known as *seeds*, are learned, population estimates are improved for unknown countries (e.g., Denmark, Russia). Individuals may abstract *statistical* information from the seeds, such as the fact that populations range from 35 million to 1 billion, which in turn helps to constrain estimates for unknown countries, or they may use specific seeds (e.g., United States) to help estimate the population of an unknown country (e.g., Russia). Man profile image copyright © John Takai. Reprinted with permission.

such as the geographic size of the countries or the population of cities within a country. The advantages of seeding are usually restricted to the specific thing you are estimating (here country populations). If you seed the knowledge base for city populations or for sizes of countries, you should get better at estimating those numbers as well. Exercise 4.3 is an application of seeding that you should have some familiarity with.

EXERCISE 4.3. The Price Is Right: Seeding the Skill of Pricing Products

Remember that seeding allows you to improve your knowledge of a domain by learning a short list of seed facts about that domain. With a small amount of seeding in a domain you can improve your ability to make estimates about a lot of other information in the domain. In this exercise, we'll show you how seeding can work for you.

Have you ever seen the TV show *The Price is Right*, where contestants need to guess the price of different merchandise? If so, how good were you when you played along with the contestants? Some people are pretty good at this game. Let's see if you can improve the skill of pricing products in the grocery store and at the same time experience the training effects of seeding.

Do you use a shopping list when you go to the store? If so, get out the list you used on your last trip to the grocery store. See what was on your list, look at what you purchased, and then try to remember or guess the price of each item. Now check yourself by getting out the actual receipt for the goods you bought. Next prepare a new shopping list for the grocery store. It will probably contain some of the same items as on your first list as well as some novel items. See how good you are at judging the prices of the items on your new list. After you finish shopping and get your receipt, you can check to see how well you did at pricing the items. You probably did

EXERCISE 4.3. The Price Is Right: Seeding the Skill of Pricing Products (*Continued*)

really well at those items that were on both your first and your second list; the difference between your estimated price and the actual price should be quite small. But how about the nonoverlapping items? How well did you do on them? Look at the nonoverlapping items on the two lists, and see whether your prices were more accurate on those nonoverlapping items for the second list than for the first list. If so, you demonstrated that seeding the knowledge base (reviewing prices for grocery items, which can only affect estimates on the second list) helped you to improve your pricing performance. You don't have to experience prices for all items in a grocery store to develop a pricing skill. A limited base of items will put you in the ballpark for just about any item in the store.

How far does seeding take you? If you seed the knowledge base for estimating the price of products at a grocery store, does it help you when you want to estimate the price of products at a hardware store? Get out a shopping list for the hardware store if you have one and try to estimate those costs. Now go shopping at the hardware store, and see how accurate your cost estimates were. Were the estimates for the hardware store less accurate than those for the nonoverlapping items on the second trip to the grocery store? If you were more accurate on nonoverlapping grocery store items than on hardware store items after seeding with grocery store items, then your pricing skill is shown to be specific to the type of product being seeded.

But if you use seeding for a variety of different stores, you should find that your general ability to estimate prices increases, so that when you enter a new type of store you should be pretty good at pricing the products there. In other words, combining seeding with variability of practice should be a very powerful way to enhance skill generalizability when it comes to the skill of pricing.

Look for Systematic Relationships (or Rules) Among Examples

We often remember specific previously encountered events. For example, from the anagram task we might later remember seeing "plape" or "rctik." For the first anagram, we might remember that the solution was "apple" and for the second "trick." Do enough of these anagrams and you should find yourself getting better and better at solving them. But you probably won't be able to remember or even recognize most of the anagrams you solved during many hours of practice. This fact is true of any skill; you will remember some but probably not all of your training experiences. Yet, you'll get better at doing the task. Rather than using your memory for previously encountered instances to improve your skill, on some occasions you can discover a general rule for responding. In the foregoing examples, there is a rule: "Reorder the anagram letters as 3-1-4-2-5." Will that rule work for all anagrams? Of course not. But it might work for the set of anagrams you're being tested on. It's worth trying to find a rule, because if you find one that does work, it will save you a lot of time and effort.

Consider a different example. Let's say that you want to improve your skill of doing mental arithmetic. In particular, perhaps you want to improve the speed and accuracy with which you can compute the product of a single-digit number and a 2-digit number (such as 5×17). Trying to memorize the answers to all possible problems of that type is an impossible task. But you might be able to master a set of rules that would give you the right answer to any problem of this type. (Consider, e.g., rules like "any digit times 10 is equal to that digit plus 0" or "any digit times 11 is equal to that digit repeated"; $5 \times 10 = 50$, $6 \times 11 = 66$.) Learning rules like these will cut down on the number of things that you have to memorize. And you will find, of course, that it is much easier to remember the rules than to remember the specific answers to all of the problems. Also, with the rules you could perform calculations outside of the range of products that you practiced (for example, you could compute the product of two 2-digit numbers). Rule use aids in all three dimensions of training—efficiency, durability, and generalizability—but it is particularly valuable for promoting generalizability, for which we don't have a lot of effective training techniques. Exercise 4.4 provides an example of how rules can be extracted from a small set of instances or problems.

Are rules facts or skills? It's a hard to say. The best answer is probably a little bit of both. If you can explicitly define a rule such as "always say 'a' before a noun that begins with a consonant sound and 'an' before a noun that begins with a vowel sound," then you know something that has the characteristics of a fact. But if you use the rule without consciously thinking much about it, it has the characteristics of a skill (or procedure). Facts are highly generalizable. Rules tend to be specific to the domain in which they apply. But, by their very nature, rules apply to many and possibly all cases of a given type within a domain. Therefore, they function at a general level. If you learn a rule, you promote generalizability. One way to enhance generalizability then is to find ways to support rule learning.

FINAL COMMENT ON GENERALIZABILITY

We have talked about three ways to promote generalizability: Change the conditions of practice, seed the knowledge base, and learn rules. Using these strategies should help ensure that what you've learned can be applied to new situations and to new tasks. Generalizability is very important because even if you have learned a skill efficiently, and even if what you've learned is durable, it might not be worth the effort for you to learn a skill if you can only apply it in limited circumstances. Recall the assertion of the eminent

EXERCISE 4.4. Deriving a Rule From Instances

During training, if you can discover and use a general rule to base your performance on, you will be able to improve the generalizability of what you have learned. You might think that rules are used only in law or in games so that rule use might not be of much help in training. But in fact rules actually occur very frequently in everyday life. Often we encounter and use rules without conscious knowledge of them. Let's consider some examples of rules of this type.

Sometimes when doing a series of problems, you can discover a rule or regularity that might apply to all the problems. This is actually quite a common experience because there are rules, either explicit or implicit, that apply to many of the everyday things that we do. Quite a few of these rules occur in language and communication because, as linguists are fond of telling us, languages are intelligible mainly because they are rule-bound. You probably can think immediately of several examples. Take the difference between "mass nouns" (like water) and "count nouns" (like tree). The rule is that mass nouns are always singular – "the water is . . ." – whereas count nouns can be either singular or plural – "the tree is . . ." and "the trees are . . ." are both acceptable. A mass noun can be preceded by "much" or "less," as in "much water," whereas a count noun in plural form takes "many" or "fewer," as in "many trees." These are hard and fast rules in English grammar that most of us learn either implicitly or explicitly as we acquire language skill.

An example of a case where you probably use a rule regularly but don't have any explicit knowledge of it has to do with the pronunciation of the definite article, "the." "The" can be pronounced either as thuh or as thee. You probably know that when you want to emphasize that word, you use the form thee. But how else do you decide what form to use? Let's go through a series of 10 nouns, in this case all names of foods, and for each one, pronounce the word "the" before it. See if you say thuh or thee, and try to determine what rule underlies the decision about which sounds better to you:

the banana
(Is it thee banana or thuh banana?)

EXERCISE 4.4. Deriving a Rule From Instances (Continued)

the apple
the orange
the grapefruit
the egg
the burger
the pea
the olive
the ice cube
the chocolate

Any ideas about the rule? Next, for the same list of nouns decide if you should say a or an before them. (A banana or an banana?) Deciding between a and an is something you do whenever you write or speak, and when to choose one word over the other is something you were probably taught in school. You use the word a before a word starting with a consonant sound, and you use the word an before a word starting with a vowel sound. So you would say "a banana," "a grapefruit," "a burger," "a pea," and "a chocolate," but you would say "an apple," "an orange," "an egg," "an olive," and "an ice cube."

The rule for deciding between thuh and thee is just the same! You say "thuh" before a word beginning with a consonant sound, and you say "thee" before a word beginning with a vowel sound. So you would say "thuh banana," "thuh grapefruit," "thuh burger," "thuh pea," and "thuh chocolate," but you would say "thee apple," "thee orange," "thee egg," "thee olive," and "thee ice cube." Most of you probably were not taught that rule in school unless you learned English as a second language. But you can find that rule in any dictionary. And even if you did not know the rule explicitly, somehow, through repeated exposures to instances, you were probably able to master the rule implicitly. Note, however, that some people who have a Southern dialect don't distinguish between thuh and thee, but pronounce "the" as thuh in all cases.

As we said, rule learning is a common phenomenon, in language and in other aspects of behavior. Rules by their very nature are generalizations. We need them if we are to get beyond being specific stimulus bound in the things that we do.

Greek philosopher Heraclitus: "No man ever steps in the same river twice." You will probably never be required to do the same task in the same context and in the same way twice. So be prepared for changes in skill requirements, and make sure that your skill training is accomplished in such a way that you can benefit from it even when the conditions of skill use do change.

THE TAKEAWAY

Acquisition of knowledge and skill takes place in a context, and retention is typically measured in the same context over the same material. If training has been successful, it should be useful in new and different situations. Surely, part of expertise is being able to use what you know when novel questions or problems arise. And training expertise is, as a bottom line, what this book is about. This chapter covers ways to train that promote generalizability. Training for generalizability is easier said than done, because acquired knowledge and skill tend to be specific to the material and the context in which learning took place.

The scientific evidence about the generalizability leg of the training stool is weaker and more limited than about the other two legs, efficiency and durability. Nonetheless, as summarized in Table 4.1, there are some techniques that work. Among them are the following:

1. Make sure that acquisition and retention sessions tap into as wide a range of material and environments as possible; in other words, practice in a variety of ways in a variety of places.
2. Seed the knowledge base. Within a given domain, a small set of well-mastered facts often provides general knowledge about the entire domain, such as the average value or the range of possible values, which can be used to inform educated judgments about other facts within that domain.

TABLE 4.1. **Training Principles for Generalizability: How to Apply What You Learn to New Situations**

Purpose: Increasing your ability to transfer what you learn to nontrained material

Principle	Application
Variability of practice	Change the conditions of practice periodically.
Seeding	Use a few selected examples to define a domain.
Rules vs. instance memory	Look for systematic relationships (or rules) among examples.

3. Look for rules and regularities among the items you've been trained on. If you find a relationship among learned items, you can often apply it successfully to novel items.

We acknowledge that there isn't much solid empirical evidence on promoting good transfer from training to novel situations. Specificity is the operative word when it comes to training. For this reason, nothing beats experience with the task in its various forms when it comes to job training. The lesson for those who design job training programs is that on-the-job training probably works best because of the range of experience it provides. There are few proven techniques to learn transferable skills. But one promising possibility is the apprenticeship model, in which a novice works with an experienced master craftsman. The supporting evidence, however, is currently lacking, and thus we can expect cognitive scientists to try to identify more successful training models as research proceeds into the future.

CHAPTER 5

REFRESHING YOUR SKILLS, AGING, AND DEBUNKING MYTHS ABOUT TRAINING

Genius is an intuitive talent for labor.

—Jan Walaeus

We conclude this book with a discussion of some additional and more general issues about training. First, we discuss the need to maintain your knowledge and skills over the long term, and how to do this. Next, we consider whether mental abilities necessarily decline with age and, if so, what can be done to mitigate the decline. Then, we debunk some common myths about self-training. Finally, we discuss new directions for the field of training.

MAINTAINING YOUR KNOWLEDGE AND SKILLS

Training effects aren't permanent. Although there are ways to train for greater durability (as shown in Chapter 3), even the best training is subject to loss over time. So, what can you do to guard against that loss?

There are two key necessities. First, maintain your motivation to perform well. You took up a training routine because you wanted to become better at something. Once you've achieved that goal, are you going to lose interest? If you do, you can expect performance to drop off and possibly reset to your pretraining level. You might think that you are unlikely to lose interest, but it could happen. If you maintain interest, you've got a leg up on performance maintenance. Second, develop a routine for refreshing your newly acquired facts and skills. Refresher practice probably does not need to be as intense as the training routine that got you to your current performance level. But it does have to be systematic and deliberate. And it will allow you to incorporate into your behavioral repertoire new developments that always come along, regardless of the area of training. Make refresher practice a part of your plans for future training. Remember, expertise is always a work in progress. To maintain their elite status, master practitioners practice their craft every day. Famous performers, like cellist Pablo Casals, work to improve their skills every day—in Casals's case, even into his 90s. As Walaeus observes in the quote at the top of this chapter, expertise rests on a talent for hard work (labor).

PREPARING FOR SOME COGNITION DECLINE WITH AGE

Even if you maintain your interest, some cognitive abilities decline in older individuals. In part, this decrease is a function of an unavoidable slowdown in reaction time and performance execution with older age, especially on tasks that are difficult to perform. Typically, the decline is reflected in the exercise of skills and less so in memory for specific facts. So, as you prepare for aging, you can expect your ability to think logically and to use what you know about the world to get a little more difficult, even though in no sense have you gotten any "dumber" or lost your general knowledge. The good news is that you can overcome this slowing-down process somewhat by continuing to do mental exercises involving speed of response on a regular basis. Practice, practice, practice—it always helps, at any age. Some researchers have described what happens with age as a loss of cognitive processing capacity, primarily skill based. Elaborating on that idea, others have suggested that your crystallized intelligence (facts that you know) remains pretty stable with age, but your fluid intelligence (skills that you know how to perform) tends to weaken. The best scientific evidence indicates that tasks involving attention, working memory (the amount of information you can keep in mind without losing track), comprehending textual material, and making logical inferences all become more difficult as you age. These mental activities all involve the ability to work with facts in the abstract, integrating what you already know into a new conclusion. One implication you can draw from these findings is that strategies to reduce the memory load of a task are likely to be of some help. For example, older adults might find it helpful to use pictures as memory aids or to be sure that the text being read for comprehension is clear and explicit. Interestingly, there is also evidence to suggest that participation in intellectually engaging activities on a daily basis can serve to buffer individuals against the decline with aging.

One of the best intellectually engaging activities is social interaction, especially one-on-one. To carry on a coherent conversation with another person, you need all of your cognitive resources, especially attention and memory, not to mention all the skills that contribute to ordinary language use.[1] If you are an older reader, you should try to keep your wits about you, to stay socially active, and, by all means, to avoid withdrawing socially or becoming a hermit in your later years.

DEBUNKING MYTHS ABOUT MIND TRAINING

Is It Possible to Train Your Brain?

Throughout this book, we have referred to training the mind—but what about the brain? The words *mind* and *brain* are sometimes

---

[1]We thank Janice Keenan for pointing out the role of cognitive processes in normal human conversation and the positive effects that social interaction and conversation can have on maintaining mental performance levels into older age.

confused or conflated. There is a common but simplistic assumption made by laypeople and scientists alike that the mind is a product of the brain and that if you really want to understand the mind, you must first understand the brain. This assumption holds that the brain explains everything we need to know about why and how we behave as we do. If we might be so bold, *this assumption is a myth*.

In this book, we have taken a different stance on the brain/mind issue. We argue that it is a person who is trained, not a brain. It is a person who learns and remembers, not a brain. The mind stands on its own, as essentially a collection of all of one's current knowledge and skill—it cannot be reduced to a single biological part. This is not to say that the brain and what goes on in the brain are irrelevant. Quite the contrary, what happens in the brain as we behave is critical to a complete understanding of the behavior. As thinking happens, so do brain processes. Mind and brain processes are time locked, and you can actually measure brain changes during thought, as shown in Figure 5.1. Still, there is no good reason to believe that brain activity causes thoughts. In fact, the reverse might be true—thoughts may cause brain activity. Or it might be the case that neither causes the other in a direct way but that both are going on at the same time in an interrelated way. Thus, mind and brain are unique but different, and both will reflect the effect that your training has on your performance. What's most important to us in this book is how your performance changes with training.

To improve performance, you need to improve your mind. Although the brain is necessary, you can't train just the brain. It is *you*—a person, complete with brain, body, and mind—that is trained to perform.

The training principles that we present in this book were developed by examining performance, not by examining the brain. We don't know where in the brain processing occurs in the training tasks we consider, and we don't know the precise neurons that might

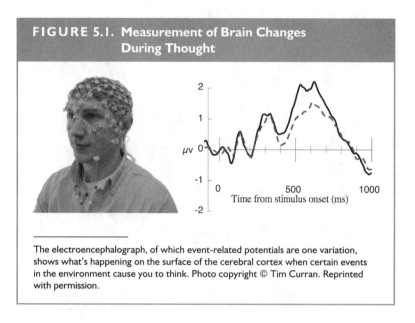

FIGURE 5.1. Measurement of Brain Changes During Thought

The electroencephalograph, of which event-related potentials are one variation, shows what's happening on the surface of the cerebral cortex when certain events in the environment cause you to think. Photo copyright © Tim Curran. Reprinted with permission.

be activated. But it doesn't matter! By examining performance during acquisition, retention, and transfer sessions, we do know ways to improve the efficiency, durability, and generalizability of your training. We have described those methods for you in the preceding chapters, and you can benefit from the principles and exercises we provided even if no one knows what's going on in your brain as you apply those methods.

Does Physical Fitness Guarantee Mental Fitness?

Physical fitness advocates often claim great benefits for mental abilities attributable to keeping the body in shape. See, for example, Media Clip 5.1 on walking and resistance training. The impression you might get from some of these claims is that it's the body that counts and that the mind is just going along for the ride. If you make

MEDIA CLIP 5.1.

Walking, Resistance Training May Improve Memory in Study

Simple exercise, such as walking and resistance training, improved thinking and memory in older adults in several new studies that suggest physical activity offers a key strategy in slowing mental decline. One trial found that walking may boost brain volume in the region for memory. Another showed that weight training helped the mental function of older women with mild cognitive impairment.

Article appeared in many newspapers on July 15, 2012. To see the full article, go to http://www.bloomberg.com/news/2012-07-15/walking-resistance-training-may-improve-memory-in-study.html.

the body strong, then simultaneously you make yourself sharper mentally. There is some truth to those claims, although it's unlikely to be a direct cause-and-effect relationship. As you become more physically fit, your general health usually improves, and you begin to "feel better." The evidence is that systematic fitness training will reduce your blood pressure, bad cholesterol, glucose levels, and obesity. Changes like those can sharpen your attention and free up your mind from all kinds of worries that tend to interfere with thinking. So, you do get a mental benefit from fitness training, but probably not in a direct way.

Further, you can get even more mental fitness benefit from training the mind. Spend the same amount of time and effort that you might invest in physical fitness training on the kind of mind training procedures outlined in this book and you'll come out far ahead mentally. In addition, the reverse may be true. Mental training might benefit your physical fitness. It's possible, although good scientific evidence is presently lacking, that developing knowledge resources and great skill in some area of training produces salutary changes in the brain, and the brain—being an organ of the body—thus benefits.

The bottom line is, mind and body are interactive, interdependent, complementary, and mutually supportive. Improving either through training benefits both.

Can Training Improve Your General Intelligence?

We know that deliberate and sustained practice on well-defined tasks, such as playing the piano or learning a language, results in steadily improving performance on those tasks. But is there any benefit from this training for cognition in general? Does your newly acquired achievement make you any better at other activities that require some of the same cognitive processes? Working memory seems to be engaged in many different types of mental activities. If we practice to improve working memory in tasks that require keeping several things in mind simultaneously, will that improvement translate to other activities, like skillfully playing bridge, that also use working memory? That is, if we engage in specialized training on working memory, will that training benefit all tasks that require working memory? Is there a general cognitive benefit to be had from training a specific memory component?

Some early results from the cognitive psychology laboratory were quite promising in this regard. Training people to remember more accurately what had happened earlier in a sequence of events appeared to result in significant improvement in a variety of tasks involving, among other things, multitasking and fluid intelligence. On the basis of these results, standardized working memory training programs were developed and have been marketed to the public as general cognitive enhancement techniques. Train your working memory and you will become better at any task that includes a significant working memory component, according to these program developers. Unfortunately, more recent studies, including some that incorporated the cognitive enhancement training programs themselves, have not been so clear-cut. When certain flaws were removed from the methods of early studies, the general improvement effects of working memory training all but disappeared. So, the issue has now become quite controversial, and we really don't know whether there is any kind of specific cognitive training, working memory or otherwise, that can produce a general enhancement of cognitive abilities. What seems to be the case, as in so many cognitive tasks that we have encountered in this book, is that training effects are pretty specific to the task trained on, and without some other kind of intervention, will not enhance performance on other tasks that seem to rely on the same cognitive processes.

Although commercially available training programs may claim to improve your general intelligence, the scientific research casts serious doubt on their effectiveness. The exercises used in these programs, much like the exercises we recommend in earlier chapters of this book, may be worthwhile, but the positive effects that you obtain are going to be specific to the tasks you practice. The tasks won't make you more intelligent in general. Furthermore, the benefits will accrue only as long as you keep up your deliberate practice routine.

What Is the Role of Multitasking in Training?

Multitasking is something that many people try to do—and many even claim to be good at it. With the availability of smartphones and other mobile devices, individuals frequently attempt to do more than one thing at a time. How often do you see people walking down the street while talking on their cell phone? How often do you see people driving a car and texting someone at the same time? How often do you see students in a class looking at their Facebook page online while they are also (ostensibly) listening to the teacher give a lecture? Events like these occur with great frequency every day. But can people really multitask successfully? Or does their performance suffer when they try to do more than one thing at a time?

Some excellent studies have shown that individuals talking on a cell phone often miss important events occurring near them that more alert individuals see. For example, in one study, a clown rode a unicycle through a college campus. Students talking on a cell phone while they walked on the same path often didn't notice this unusual event even when it occurred right next to or in front of them!

As mentioned in the discussion of the functional task in Chapter 3, driving a car while talking on a cell phone, or even worse, while texting, impairs driving as much as being intoxicated would. It increases the likelihood of erratic driving, of missing important road signs or traffic lights, and of being involved in an accident. Another demonstration of what has come to be called *inattentional blindness* comes from a recent investigation of students in science classes at a major university, which showed that those students who used their cell phone during class—for example, to text a friend— had significantly lower grades (by .36 on a 4-point scale) than did the students who refrained from doing so. The authors of this study concluded that no one—not students or anyone else—can multitask as effectively as they think they can.

The detrimental effects of multitasking are becoming widely known. The cartoon *Dilbert* even pokes fun at the boss's inability to multitask—see Figure 5.2. On a more serious note, the following tragic story about an air traffic controller shows that multitasking can have critical, and sometimes fatal, consequences. This controller often had to pay attention to the radio frequency of two aircraft at the same time. To do so, he had to switch his physical position and his attention back and forth between two workstations. Usually,

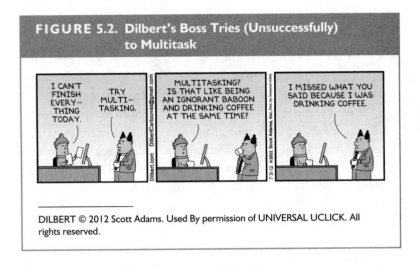

FIGURE 5.2. Dilbert's Boss Tries (Unsuccessfully) to Multitask

this switching back and forth was doable. However, one day the controller had to use the telephone and found it was not working:

> A multitasking situation emerged. Preoccupied with trying to contact the airport, distracted by the presence of technicians in the room, and burdened by having to visually scan two radar screens projecting images at significantly different scales, he inadvertently "dropped" the act of monitoring the aircraft, therefore failing to notice that two of them were actually on a collision course. Sadly, on that day the last thread of hope, a ground-based collision warning system, also happened to be switched off for maintenance. Simply following standard air traffic control procedures was not sufficient to prevent the controller from making a fatal mistake, and the two aircraft collided in midair killing all aboard.[2]

---

[2]Quoted passage on page 299. Barshi, I., & Loukopoulos, L. (2012). Training for real-world job performance. In A. F. Healy & L. E. Bourne, Jr. (Eds.), *Training cognition: Optimizing efficiency, durability, and generalizability* (pp. 287–306). New York, NY: Psychology Press.

Don't be deluded into thinking that you can perform any two tasks simultaneously and handle them equally well just because you're skilled at both. Like it or not, you (indeed, all human beings) have limited mental processing capacity. If that capacity is exceeded, which is pretty easy to do, one or the other task, and maybe both, will suffer.

When you do training involving reading, writing, or arithmetic, do you do it with music, the radio, or TV on in the background? Again, listening to music while training requires multitasking, which usually results in poorer performance on one or the other (or both) tasks.

But, in fact, there are occasions when two tasks can be done at the same time without a significant loss in performance on either. In those cases, one of the tasks is done at a high level of skill, requiring little if any conscious attention. For example, washing dishes while listening to music probably won't result in poor performance because most people are skilled enough at washing dishes that a little musical distraction won't hinder their performance. However, if attention and working memory are required for both tasks, then they cannot be done simultaneously without a deficit in performance on at least one of the tasks. Even with much experience multitasking, such costs are inevitable. Therefore, in training, if you're serious about it, we recommend that you avoid trying to do two or more things at the same time.

WHAT'S IN THE FUTURE FOR TRAINING?

Ways to train most effectively have not been completely nailed down. Most of the training principles described in this book come from research done over the past 30 or so years, primarily by psychologists. The research has been conducted in the laboratory, and it has produced principles and techniques that are well established scientifically. But research goes on, motivated primarily by a genuine scientific interest in human learning, memory, and cognition and by the practical job training needs that arise in industry, in the military, and in other walks of life. We expect to know more as time goes by and to be able to expand the number of procedures we can recommend to anyone interested in improving performance on activities that require a sharp mind. As this book ends, let's consider a couple of areas in which a better understanding of training is likely to develop in the near future.

Using Digital Technology

Self-training will benefit from advances in digital technology. The impact is already apparent. You can use digital devices to create tasks like vocabulary learning, typing, or data entry that are the basis of several exercises. Laptops and iPads are excellent for keeping performance records and analyzing them so as to produce individualized learning curves (see the discussion of learning curves in Chapter 1). Feedback on performance accuracy can be made readily available on computer screens. We expect to see online courses become available wherein you might be able to train yourself at home on some type of musical instrument or acquire a new language or learn the fundamentals of electronics.

In the online class, you can benefit not only from individualized feedback on your performance but also from the implementation of what has come to be called *clicker technology*. As used in the classroom, this technology employs handheld devices, or clickers, given to each student. The instructor periodically interrupts study activities with multiple-choice questions, and students respond to the questions by pressing one of five buttons on the clicker. Students' responses are usually made anonymously, but students are often shown on a slide how many of them have selected each alternative in a given multiple-choice question. This enables them to see whether they gave the same response as their peers. But clicker technology can be applied in the self-help online training situation, with individual trainees entering their answers to periodic questions and receiving feedback after responses from all trainees have been entered. The technique has a number of benefits that capitalize on the training principles we discussed earlier in this book. Foremost among them is the fact that the clicker technique involves frequent testing. As discussed previously, testing has been shown to be the most effective way to promote learning of material, even more effective than directly studying the material. With or without the clicker, you can provide for periodic self-testing in your own acquisition, retention, and transfer sessions (though without the clicker methodology you won't get the benefit of knowing how others are doing on the same test).

Rehabilitation Training

Our primary focus in this book is on training routines intended to enhance the performance of a normal healthy individual. An interesting question that arises is whether the routines that have been demonstrated to be effective for normal people are also effective for people who, for reasons of brain damage or loss of limbs, have difficulty doing even the most routine mental or physical tasks. To what extent is it possible to retrain a person after injury to do things that he or she was once able to accomplish, and do the same principles work in retraining that are successful in initial training? This question has gained public interest recently because of brain injuries resulting from the wartime activities of our military personnel, concussions in contact sports like football and hockey, and gunshot wounds suffered by prominent civilians like James Brady and Gabrielle Giffords.

First, of course, the body has to recover to the extent possible. Damage to the brain and other vital organs doesn't magically correct itself. Perhaps medication will accelerate the recovery process, but, at present, supporting evidence for that possibility is weak or nonexistent. See, for example, Media Clip 5.2 on treatment for brain injury. Recovery takes time and expert medical care. When the body is ready, it is time for deliberate, repetitive, drill-like practice,

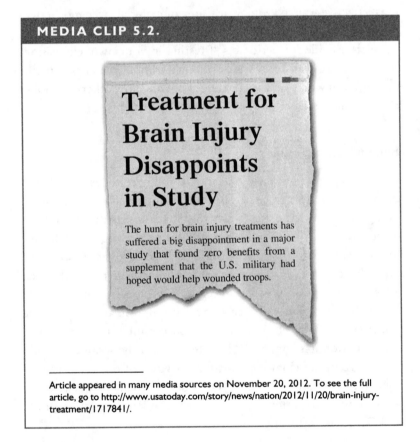

MEDIA CLIP 5.2.

Treatment for Brain Injury Disappoints in Study

The hunt for brain injury treatments has suffered a big disappointment in a major study that found zero benefits from a supplement that the U.S. military had hoped would help wounded troops.

Article appeared in many media sources on November 20, 2012. To see the full article, go to http://www.usatoday.com/story/news/nation/2012/11/20/brain-injury-treatment/1717841/.

practice, practice. This is pretty much the same formula that works for initial training. The focus has to be on rebuilding the necessary knowledge and skill sets. In fact, the major emphasis in retraining has to be on skill building, because often the required knowledge seems still to be there, although latent. Having a retrainer will be absolutely essential, at least in the beginning. The retrainer will concentrate on reestablishing skills like memory retrieval that contribute to the expression of knowledge in performance. Nobody is saying that it will be easy or that rehabilitation can get someone all the way back to normal. A review of the scientific literature on cognitive rehabilitation, though, shows that deficit-specialized rehabilitation programs do lead to significant behavioral improvements.

We hope, of course, that you will never have the need for cognitive rehabilitation. We discuss the issue here for two reasons: first, to point out that training can be effective in restoring at least some abilities, and second, to identify an area of training research in which interest is likely to grow in the near future.

THE TAKEAWAY

In this chapter, we have examined a number of issues that extend beyond training for improved mental performance. Foremost is the issue of maintenance of acquired performance levels. If you want to remain at the peak of your game, you'll need to continue your hard work. Training requires periodic refreshing, but of course at this point you'll be getting a lot of reinforcement from just doing well. We also need to recognize that abilities tend to wane with age. The human body doesn't usually last for 100 years, and it shows signs of wearing out in later decades of life. Likewise, the mind deteriorates, so maintenance of knowledge and skill through continued practice is especially important as we age. Finally, we debunked some common myths about self-training, such as the myth that physical fitness necessarily leads to mental fitness, the myth that training on particular tasks can improve your general intelligence, and the myth that people can multitask without their performance suffering.

Is this the end of the mind-training story? Of course, there is more to it. We've already noted how different domains of expertise, different people, and different goals in life all require tweaking or adjustments to the training routine for optimal effects. To present that level of detail, however, would necessitate a much longer book. We have tried to give you the essentials of training. If you have found them effective for your purpose, you should have no trouble adapting them to your own particular needs.

There's a saying that only three things matter when it comes to buying or selling real estate: location, location, location. When it comes to training, what matters most is practice, practice, practice. Practice underlies the acquisition of new knowledge and skills, helps to ensure that they are durable over time, and promotes their transfer to every new situation. With that caveat, we wish you every success in your next training adventure.

RECOMMENDED ADDITIONAL READING

Ambrose, S. A., Bridges, M. W., DiPietro, M., Lovett, M. C., & Norman, M. K. (2010). *How learning works: Seven research-based principles for smart teaching.* San Francisco, CA: Jossey-Bass.

Practical applications of research on fact learning for the classroom are described. Extensive literature reviews are provided, along with suggestions about how to improve your teaching methods.

Bushman, B. (Ed.). (2011). *ACSM's complete guide to fitness and health.* New York, NY: Human Kinetics.

There are many good books on fitness and body training. This one is a compilation of well-established and empirically supported techniques, prepared by the American College of Sports Medicine. You can find just about anything you need in the way of training exercises in this guide.

Clark, R. C. (2008). *Building expertise: Cognitive methods for training and performance improvement* (3rd ed.). San Francisco, CA: Pfeiffer/Wiley.

This book describes principles that might be used by instructional professionals to build innovative forms of expertise. The focus is on guidelines for course designers that are based on psychological evidence, rather than on self-help exercises. It provides practical recommendations for problem-centered instruction.

Healy, A. F., & Bourne, L. E., Jr. (2012). *Training cognition: Efficiency, durability, and generalizability.* New York, NY: Psychology Press.

A review of contemporary experimental and theoretical literature on training, including some possible applications of these basic cognitive scientific results. A set of previously unpublished laboratory experiments is also included.

Loukopoulos, L. D., Dismukes, R. K., & Barshi, I. (2009). *The multitasking myth: Handling complexity in real-world operations.* Aldershot, England: Ashgate.

A discussion of multitasking requirements faced by pilots. This description of the dynamic procedures followed by pilots and the concurrent interruptions and demands encountered by them makes it clear that individuals must often do multiple things at the same time but that such multitasking can lead to serious errors or accidents.

Marcus, G. (2012). *Guitar zero.* New York, NY: Penguin Group.

Gary Marcus took up the guitar later in life and demonstrates that it is never too late to develop a complex new skill. This case study of training and expertise shows how motivation and deliberate practice can overcome the limitations that sometimes accompany aging. http://www.npr.org/books/authors/145461512/gary-marcus

McDaniel, M. A., Maier, S. F., & Einstein, G. O. (2002). "Brain-specific" nutrients: A memory cure? *Psychological Science in the Public Interest, 3,* 12–38.

A review and evaluation of research on nutrition and its role in cognition. Claims that some nutrients can enhance memory or protect against memory loss are outlined, and the empirical evidence to support those claims is assessed. The bottom line is that very few sound positive data are found in the literature.

Miller, G. A. (1992). *Psychology: The science of mental life.* New York, NY: Longmans.

An introduction to psychology as an academic discipline. Something of an antidote to (a) behaviorism, the dominant school of thought in psychology during the first 50 years of the 20th century that eschewed any cognitive component of human behavior, and (b) neuroscience and its explanation of human behavior purely by neurological mechanisms. According to Miller, psychology stands as a science on its own two feet, with plenty of rigor and rapidly accumulating data.

Restak, R., & Kim, S. (2010). *The playful brain.* New York, NY: Riverhead Books.

A very readable, highly entertaining exposition on mental puzzles and how working on them can lead to a skilled level of performance. The theme is that puzzle practice changes your brain, which in turn produces performance changes. The range of puzzles presented and the information on how they tie into cognitive processes are excellent. Only intuition, though, not science, supports the further argument that it all comes down to corresponding changes in the brain.

Simon, H. (1969). *The sciences of the artificial.* Cambridge, MA: MIT Press. In this classic monograph, Nobel Prize winner Herb Simon makes a case for how much knowledge a person must have to qualify as an expert in some domains such as chess. Simon estimates an expert's knowledge to be 50,000 chunks of information.

BIBLIOGRAPHY

Brown, N. R., & Siegler, R. S. (1996). Long-term benefits of seeding the knowledge base. *Psychonomic Bulletin & Review, 3,* 385–388. doi:10.3758/BF03210766

Crutcher, R. J., & Healy, A. F. (1989). Cognitive operations and the generation effect. *Journal of Experimental Psychology: Learning, Memory, and Cognition, 15,* 669–675. doi:10.1037/0278-7393.15.4.669

Driskell, J. E., Willis, R. P., & Copper, C. (1992). Effect of overlearning on retention. *Journal of Applied Psychology, 77,* 615–622. doi:10.1037/0021-9010.77.5.615

Duncan, D. K., Hoekstra, A. R., & Wilcox, B. R. (2012). Digital devices, distraction, and student performance: Does in-class cell phone use reduce learning? *Astronomy Education Review, 11,* 010108. doi:10.3847/AER2012011

Ericsson, K. A., Chase, W. G., & Faloon, S. (1980). Acquisition of a memory skill. *Science, 208,* 1181–1182. doi:10.1126/science.7375930

Healy, A. F., Wohldmann, E. L., & Bourne, L. E., Jr. (2005). The procedural reinstatement principle: Studies on training, retention, and transfer. In A. F. Healy (Ed.), *Experimental cognitive psychology and its applications* (pp. 59–71). Washington, DC: American Psychological Association. doi:10.1037/10895-005

Healy, A. F., Wohldmann, E. L., Parker, J. T., & Bourne, L. E., Jr. (2005). Skill training, retention, and transfer: The effects of a concurrent secondary task. *Memory & Cognition, 33,* 1457–1471. doi:10.3758/BF03193378

Hyman, I. E., Jr., Boss, S. M., Wise, B. M., McKenzie, K. E., & Caggiano, J. M. (2010). Did you see the unicycling clown? Inattentional blindness while walking and talking on a cell phone. *Applied Cognitive Psychology, 24,* 597–607. doi:10.1002/acp.1638

Kerr, R., & Booth, B. (1978). Specific and varied practice of motor skill. *Perceptual and Motor Skills, 46,* 395–401.

Kole, J. A., & Healy, A. F. (2007). Using prior knowledge to minimize interference when learning large amounts of information. *Memory & Cognition, 35,* 124–137. doi:10.3758/BF03195949

Kole, J. A., Healy, A. F., & Bourne, L. E., Jr. (2008). Cognitive complications moderate the speed–accuracy tradeoff in data entry: A cognitive antidote to inhibition. *Applied Cognitive Psychology, 22,* 917–937. doi:10.1002/acp.1401

Miller, G. A. (1956). The magical number seven, plus or minus two: Some limits on our capacity for processing information. *Psychological Review, 63,* 81–97. doi:10.1037/h0043158

Mrazek, M. D., Franklin, M. S., Phillips, D. T., Baird, B., & Schooler, J. W. (2013). Mindfulness training improves working memory capacity and GRE performance while reducing mind wandering. *Psychological Science, 24,* 776–781. doi:10.1177/0956797612459659

Rabipour, S., & Raz, A. (2012). Training the brain: Fact and fad in cognitive and behavioral remediation. *Brain and Cognition, 79,* 159–179. doi:10.1016/j.bandc.2012.02.006

Roediger, H. L., III, & Karpicke, J. D. (2006). The power of testing memory: Basic research and implications for educational practice. *Perspectives on Psychological Science, 1,* 181–210. doi:10.1111/ j.1745-6916.2006.00012.x

Schmidt, R. A., & Bjork, R. A. (1992). New conceptualizations of practice: Common principles in three paradigms suggest new concepts for training. *Psychological Science, 3,* 207–217. doi:10.1111/j.1467-9280. 1992.tb00029.x

Schmidt, R. A., Young, D. E., Swinnen, S., & Shapiro, D. C. (1989). Summary knowledge of results for skill acquisition: Support for the guidance hypothesis. *Journal of Experimental Psychology: Learning, Memory, and Cognition, 15,* 352–359. doi:10.1037/0278-7393.15.2.352

Shipstead, Z., Redick, T. S., & Engle, R. W. (2012). Is working memory training effective? *Psychological Bulletin, 138,* 628–654. doi:10.1037/ a0027473

Wickens, C., Hutchins, S., Carolan, T., & Cumming, J. (2012). Attention and cognitive resource load in training strategies. In A. F. Healy & L. E., Bourne, Jr. (Eds.), *Training cognition: Optimizing efficiency, durability, and generalizability* (pp. 67–88). New York, NY: Psychology Press.

Wohldmann, E. L., Healy, A. F., & Bourne, L. E., Jr. (2008). A mental practice superiority effect: Less retroactive interference and more transfer than physical practice. *Journal of Experimental Psychology: Learning, Memory, and Cognition, 34,* 823–833. doi:10.1037/0278-7393.34.4.823

INDEX

Accuracy, 40
Acquisition sessions
  activities in, 16, 46
  context of, 98
  feedback during, 24
  zone of learnability within, 28–31
Age
  and cognitive decline, 102–103
  for mental training, 5–6
Anagrams, 87–88, 94
Antiques Roadshow (TV show), 81–83
Associations, 54, 55, 57, 71
Attention, 103, 111. *See also* Focus, of attention

Barshi, I., 110n2
Blindness, inattentional, 109
Body, the, 3–4
  injuries to, 113–114
  mental training role of, 105–107
  physical exercise, 12–13, 105–107
Bodybuilding, 12
Boredom, 14–15, 39–40, 43
Bourne, L. E., Jr., 21n2
Brady, James, 113
Brain. *See also* Mental training
  and mind/brain issue in training, 103–105
  and rehabilitation training, 113–115

Casals, Pablo, 102
Categorical organization, 47
Cerebral cortex, 105
Cervantes, Miguel de, 45
Chunking (memory strategy), 60–63, 79
Clicker technology, 112–113
Coaches, 12–13
Cognitive antidote, 15, 40, 43
Cognitive decline, 102–103
Cognitive psychology, ix
Commitment, 8
Complications, in training tasks, 46–50, 79
Comprehension, 103
Crossword puzzles, 3
Crystallized intelligence, 102–103

Declarative information, 62, 64
Deep training, 67, 79
Deliberate practice, 7
"Desirable difficulties," 46
Dietary changes, 12
Digital technology, 112–113
Digit span, 51–52
Dilbert, 7, 8, 109–110
Domains of knowledge, 90
Drugs, nonprescription, 10–12

ABOUT THE AUTHORS

Lyle E. Bourne, Jr., PhD, is Professor Emeritus and former chairman of the Department of Psychology and former director of the Institute of Cognitive Science at the University of Colorado. He has served as president of the Rocky Mountain Psychological Association; president of the Federation of Cognitive, Psychological, and Behavioral Sciences; and president of both the Division of Experimental Psychology (Division 3) and the Society of General Psychology (Division 1) of the American Psychological Association. He can be reached at lyle.bourne@colorado.edu.

Alice F. Healy, PhD, is College Professor of Distinction and director of the Center for Research on Training at the University of Colorado. She has served as editor of *Memory & Cognition*, chair of the Psychology Section of the American Association for the Advancement of Science, president of the Rocky Mountain Psychological Association, president of the Division of Experimental Psychology (Division 3) of the American Psychological Association, and chair of the Society of Experimental Psychologists. She can be reached at alice.healy@colorado.edu.